How to Invest in Real Estate Syndicates

How to Invest in Real Estate Syndicates

DANIEL A. MILLER

DOW JONES-IRWIN
Homewood, Illinois 60430

This publication is designed to provide accurate and authoritative information in regard to the subject matter covered. It is sold with the understanding that the publisher is not engaged in rendering legal, accounting, or other professional service. If legal advice or other expert assistance is required, the services of a competent professional person should be sought.

From a Declaration of Principles jointly adopted by a Committee of the American Bar Association and a Committee of Publishers.

ISBN 0-87094-162-3
Library of Congress Catalog Card No. 78–446

Printed in the United States of America

2 3 4 5 6 7 8 9 0 K 5 4 3 2 1 0 9

This book is dedicated
to my wife, Monique,
and to my son, Brandon.

Preface

This book was written to provide real estate syndicate investors, as well as financial advisors, with the tools necessary to evaluate the risks and benefits of any real estate offering. To do so, the book covers five important areas:

1. *Syndicate organization and economics.* How and why syndicate investments can earn you substantial profits. The tax benefits of syndicate investment. How syndicates are structured.
2. *The syndicate manager.* How to choose a syndicator. How to assess syndication fees and their impact on the investment.
3. *The syndicate property.* How you can analyze and evaluate the syndicate property's advantages, disadvantages, and economic value.
4. *Investor safeguards.* How you can protect yourself against the risks of syndication. Rights and remedies you can exercise if things go wrong.
5. *Syndicate investment strategies.* Proper strategies to carry out the advice given.

As you read, you will see that several important themes are explicitly and implicitly threaded through each section:

When you consider various investment possibilities, safety and security must be considered just as important as glamor and profits. Your eye should always be on the basic economic soundness of the investment, not just on the tax benefits promised. Tax write-offs of several thousand dollars will serve no purpose if you stand to lose the tens of thousands of dollars you have invested. You should trust your money only to proven and experienced syndicators. The syndicate's structure should provide ample financial incentives for the syndicator to be conscientious in the acquisition, management, and resale of the syndicate property. Before you invest money, you must invest time and effort to ferret out all the facts and figures you will need to make an informed judgment about the investment.

Even if you follow this book's recommendations to the letter, you should seek additional help and guidance from professionals—real estate brokers, real estate management firms, your lawyer, your accountant.

Finally, you must always remember that there is no such thing as a "perfect" investment. Even the best-designed syndicate will have its risks. It is up to you to put them all in proper perspective.

May 1978 **Daniel A. Miller**

Special Acknowledgment

I wish to express my gratitude to John Fried, not only for editing this book, but also for assisting me in transforming many difficult legal and financial concepts and structures into comprehendable written form.

Contents

Introduction: What This Book Will Do for You

Slumped low into the leather Danish chair in front of my desk and staring through the window of the office, Dr. John Forester was a study in sullen moodiness. It was our second meeting.

"I put half my life savings into that syndicate," he had told me about a week earlier. "The property looked great. For two years I've been getting letters from the syndicator telling me how well the property was doing. I got one less than a month ago."

"And you had no idea your investment was in trouble?"

"None," he had answered. "Not until I got the notice that the property was in foreclosure. How could things go sour so quickly?"

Hoping to get some idea why his investment had deteriorated, I had asked Dr. Forester some rather simple (I thought) questions. He could answer none.

"How many other investors are involved?"

"I have no idea."

"Well, do you know who holds legal title to the property?"

"No. The syndicate, I would think. Shouldn't it?"

By now, I was getting a little bit annoyed myself.

"Have you ever seen a tax return for the partnership?"

"No. Never."

"Okay. Do you at least know what the unpaid balance on the mortgage is? Who is foreclosing?"

Dr. Forester just shook his head.

Now, at this meeting, Dr. Forester was deeply upset because I was giving him a detailed report of what a cursory investigation of the situation had revealed.

"Usually," I explained to him, "a syndicator will find a desirable property, negotiate on an arm's length basis for its purchase, tie it down with an escrow deposit, and then will find investors quickly who will contribute the capital needed to close the purchase of the property.

"But in your case, the syndicator purchased the property himself from a syndicator who was his friend and who made a profit on the sale. Then your syndicator turned right around and sold the building to your syndicate at an additional increase in price. In dollars that means that the first syndicator bought the building for $700,000, resold it to your syndicator for $800,000, and your syndicator sold it to your syndicate for $900,000."

Dr. Forester just blinked.

"Not only that, but both sales of property were made under what we call an unrecorded contract of sale."

"And what does that mean?"

"That the syndicate never really held title to the property. Legal record title is still in the first syndicator's name."

"Now I am confused. Why is the bank foreclosing on us? Why doesn't it foreclose on the syndicator?"

I took a deep breath before telling him the really bad news. "Well, there is no bank foreclosing on the property. It's the first syndicator himself. What he is doing, is moving to repossess the property."

When I saw the look on Dr. Forester's face, I was glad the windows in my office were hermetically sealed.

"But, I don't. . . ."

"Unfortunately, it's simple. First of all, not only did both syndicators make a profit by selling the property, but your syndicator also paid himself a real estate commission from the capital he raised from you and the others. That commission, and the fact that the price had been marked up so drastically meant that a large amount of money was needed to finance the purchase. In fact, the difference between the $700,000 which the first syndicator paid for the building and the $900,000 your syndicate paid, was financed by two separate $100,000 loans in favor of each syndicator.

"Now, under *any* circumstances, the apartment building could not have generated sufficient income to cover the various loan payments the syndicate now owed. Also, out of the rental income, your syndicator has also been taking a cut as a management fee, so the margin between operating costs and revenues grew even wider. Inevitably something had to give since there was not enough money to go around.

"Naturally, your syndicator decided that he was not going to be the one left out in the cold. So, he did a simple thing. Out of the insufficient revenues he made the loan payments due him. But he did not pay his friend, the first syndicator. And, the first syndicator took the only avenue open to him. He foreclosed on your syndicate's property."

Fortunately, the story had a semihappy ending. Dr. Forester and his fellow investors, aided by legal counsel, confronted both syndicators. Because they had engaged in a good bit of chicanery, the syndicators were financially and legally exposed. They did not have enough money to make full restitution. However, they had just enough to pay back half of Dr. Forester's original investment before their empires collapsed.

Dr. Forester's case was not all that uncommon. The number of investors financially wounded by bad real estate syndicate investments is legion. And, while it may sound cruel, in the vast majority of cases, they have no one to blame but themselves. True, real estate syndicates have proliferated and grown increasingly complex. And no real estate investment, no matter how conservative or well managed, is completely risk-free. But investors, including men and women who are trained professionals and who have reached upper echelons in their fields, seldom take more than a cursory look at the syndicate they are considering. They ask "How much do I stand to make? What will my tax write-offs be?" And then leave it at that.

To make money in real estate syndication—and I must say that a syndicate investment can be a highly lucrative undertaking for you—and to avoid the considerable pitfalls in the field, you must be willing to do some basic research. Moreover, you must know what you are looking for, what questions to ask, how to judge the answers you get, what risks you should consider taking, and which ones to avoid. This book will teach you how to do these things through investor checklists, case studies, and hypothetical examples. As a result, you will be able to maximize syndicate investment profits and minimize syndicate investment risks.

1

How Real Estate Syndicates Make Profits

In most every part of the nation—whether in California, Chicago, or on the East Coast—real estate prices are on a virtual forced march upward.

While a fascination with property ownership and investment is an American tradition of long standing, the current and continuing escalation in real estate values has reinforced, if not accelerated, this desire to own real property—be it a small lot, a modest apartment building, or a large office complex. Day by day, an increasing number of men and women are buying into one of the most exciting bull real estate markets of recent history.

There are, of course, many ways in which an individual can funnel money into real estate. But within the last years, an increasing number of people have come to depend on real estate syndicates to handle their investments.

What is a real estate syndicate? In essence, it is an organizational structure in which capital—supplied by a group of investors who have money but not the time, desire, or knowledge to dabble actively in real estate ventures—is married to the managerial skills offered by a person (or persons) able to organize the syndicate, to find suitable property, to negotiate for its acquisition, and to manage it until it is sold. Real estate syndicates are formed to invest in apartment buildings, office buildings, and new construction projects; to rehabilitate older properties; and to convert properties from one use to another. Syndicates are formed to buy shopping centers, mobile home parks, condominiums, and hotels. Their diversity and versatility, in other words, is virtually unlimited.

Any sound real estate investment will yield significant advantages. It can provide the investor with a steady flow of spendable cash—the money left over from revenues after cash disbursements have been made for operating the property and for paying the mortgage. Depreciation write-offs, whether taken evenly over the useful life of the property or accelerated to provide greater tax advantages in the early years of the investment, provide the "paper" losses which are the basis for legitimate federal and state tax deductions and the pillars of the tax shelters used to protect from taxation some of the investor's income from other sources. And, a good real estate investment will, under most circumstances, yield the equity buildup, appreciation in value, and hedge against inflation that any intelligent investor expects.

BENEFITS OF SYNDICATION

Financial Leverage

The benefits of real estate ownership can be magnified greatly by participation in a syndicate. An individual investor, looking for a piece of property, may find that the really choice opportunities are too expensive. A syndicate, on the other hand, allows a group of investors to pool their funds to buy the larger, often better, properties. And because larger properties can usually be purchased with a smaller proportional cash down payment than smaller properties, the syndicate (and by extension the individual investor) gets more for the money. Finally, because large properties require high cash outlays, fewer buyers usually compete to buy them. As a result, there is more room for bargaining, an advantage competent syndicate managers are quick to exploit.

As a result of the financial leverage that accrues to syndicates, an investor can purchase "more" real estate through the syndicate than he could by himself. Furthermore, the better financial leverage ultimately means better tax benefits. This in turn means greater profits per invested dollar. It is not uncommon, for example, for a syndicate to acquire a $1 million apartment building with a 15 percent ($150,000) cash down payment. Let us compare this to a single investor who purchases a $250,000 apartment building, but is required to make a 25 percent ($62,500) down payment. If we assume that the purchase price of both properties is allocated 80 percent to the building and 20 percent to the land, and that each property has a 20-year depreciable life, then the depreciation tax benefits for the two properties are as follows:

a. $1 million property. $40,000 a year depreciation ($800,000, credited to the building, divided by 20). This results in a yearly tax write-off attributable to depreciation of 26.66 percent on the syndicate's joint capital ($40,000/$150,000). The full 26.66 percent, of course, flows through to the individual investors.

b. $250,000 property. $10,000 a year depreciation ($200,000, credited to the building, divided by 20). This results in a yearly tax write-off attributable to depreciation of 16 percent on the lone investor's capital ($10,000/$62,500).

The syndication process, in other words, offers its investors the opportunity to gain an additional 10 percent tax deduction each year because of the better leverage available to the syndicate. If we assume that investors in real estate syndicates are likely to be men and women in the 50 percent tax bracket (or more) the additional tax benefit results in an annual equivalent of 5 percent (or more) cash return during the entire term of the investment.

To carry our example one step further, let's see what happens if the lone investor and the syndicate each resell their buildings three years later for 15 percent more than they paid for them.

a. $1 million property. Resold at $1,150,000. The syndicate receives $150,000 profit on its original capital investment of $150,000, or 100 percent return on its investment.

b. $250,000 property. Resold at $287,500. The lone investor receives $37,500 profit on the original capital investment of $62,500—a mere 60 percent return on his or her investment.

Again, financial leverage has carried the day! The syndicate investors receive 40 percent more on their investment.[1]

Economies of Size

The leverage that allows you, as an investor in a syndicate, to buy into a larger property than would be possible if you were to invest in real estate by yourself, yields an additional bonus—a potentially greater cash return on your investment.

This greater cash flow comes about because large properties bring so-called economies of size with them. For example, a 40-unit apartment building and a 10-unit building may both have a swimming pool that costs $1,000 a year to maintain. If you were to buy the ten-unit building by yourself and if your yearly rental income were to be $25,000, the maintenance of the pool would be costing you about 4 percent of that income a year. But if you had the financial wherewithal to buy the 40-unit building that had yearly rental income of $100,000, the cost of pool maintenance would represent a mere 1 percent of the rents—and more money would be flowing into your pockets. Similarly, because syndicates can buy larger buildings and because maintenance of crucial amenities such as pools, elevators, saunas, and Jacuzzis, represents a proportionately smaller part of rental income, the net cash flow to the syndicate —and to you—is larger.

Expertise of the Syndicator

Not too long ago, a doctor I knew decided that his high income needed the benefits of a tax shelter. Specifically, he wanted to find a way to cut his taxable income by a full $50,000.

Because he had picked up a little knowledge about real estate in cocktail party conversations with lawyers and account-

[1] You should be advised, however, that financial leverage can be a two-edged sword. Since higher leverage results in higher mortgage loan payments, adverse rental market conditions can seriously affect highly leveraged properties with financially unstable tenants. Therefore, highly leveraged investments are feasible only when the properties are well located and have strong, stable tenants.

ant friends, he decided that the best way to achieve his goal would be to buy an apartment building, pick up the mortgage, and prepay $50,000 in interest in the year he bought the property. When he found what he was looking for, he rushed into the deal. He made a $50,000 down payment plus paid an *additional* $50,000 in prepaid interest.

He was very proud of his little coup—until he told me the story of his venture. I had to tell him that he did not have to spend $100,000 in order to buy the property and reach his tax goals.

If he had found a syndicator knowledgeable in tax law, I told the doctor, he could have invested just $50,000 and would have achieved all he set out to do.

The doctor's experience has a moral. The lone investor seldom has the knowledge and sophistication to put together the kind of property venture that will yield the greatest benefits for the least dollars. The parallel lesson is this: The investor who joins a syndicate gains the expertise of people who have the skill and the experience to develop the complex and innovative real estate deals that can confer the considerable tax advantages and safeguards the investor seeks—without tying up more of the investor's money than absolutely necessary.

(In fact, we can take the doctor's experience further and learn still another moral. It is unwise to invest, whether alone or as part of a syndicate, in property for only its purported tax benefits. The worst piece of property can be bought in a way that will provide high tax write-offs. Property should only be bought for tax benefits if, in addition, it has a sound economic future. Moreover, the tax benefits should be considered with an eye toward the Internal Revenue Service. Is this agency likely to accept the specific tax claims made in the wake of the deal?)

Limited Liability

One of the primary benefits of a syndicate investment is that it offers each individual investor limited liability. A member of a syndicate cannot be held personally liable for any of the obligations incurred by the syndicate or the syndicator. Thus, if you invest $5,000 in a syndicate and if the property racks up debts of $50,000, or goes into foreclosure, all you stand to lose is your initial $5,000 contribution. Creditors have no recourse against you personally.

Passive Ownership

Again, an object lesson: I have a friend, an accountant, who bought an apartment building and then hired an inexperienced resident manager to handle the day-to-day operations of the property.

Within a very short time, trouble reared its head. Annoyed by the novice manager's inability to handle their problems, renters began to move out. Income from the property began to drop. Because the manager did not have the skills necessary to keep the building in good repair, operating expenses began to soar as plumbers and electricians came to call on a regular basis. In order to salvage his investment, my friend had to move into the apartment building and take over its management. While he did get things back on an even keel, it was only at a price. My friend had to cut way back on the hours he could devote to this profession. As a result, income from his accounting practice fell drastically.

Property management, in other words, requires a considerable amount of time, skill, and effort. Simply put, it involves a never-ending procession of "headaches." Thus, syndicates offer another advantage. The syndicator or syndicators assume the responsibility for the tiresome day-to-day management crises, thereby allowing the investor the opportunity to own property —without being owned by it.

Broader Investment Base

The lone investor with $100,000 to spare is, all too often, tempted to sink everything into a single real estate venture. If the venture fails, the investor can lose every penny. But real estate syndication offers a practical alternative to the pitfalls of all-or-nothing investments. The investor could put $10,000 into each of ten different syndications. Should any one of the syndications fail—and like any other business ventures, a syndication can indeed come a cropper—the individual investor has lost only a portion of his capital.

RISKS OF SYNDICATE INVESTMENTS

Lack of Control and Information

As might be expected, syndicates have disadvantages as well, often directly derived from the very benefits discussed above.

Because syndicate participation is essentially passive, the individual investor has little or no control over the property held. For example, the property is generally resold or refinanced when the syndicate's organizers think it is appropriate to do so. Thus, the individual investor may find that the syndicators have decided to sell the property because a huge profit is in the offing. And yet, that large profit may come in a year when the investor has already earned a good deal of money. The investor may very well have preferred to have the syndicate investment gains come in another year.

While a syndicate investment will put a protective cushion between the investor and the daily aggravations of property management, the passive nature of the syndicate investment can work to keep the investor *too much in the dark.* Not that the small flow of information from syndicator to investor is willful, but even the most reliable syndicate organizer will often be too busy to keep the investors informed of every little event that occurs while the investment is active.

Thus, the person who joins a real estate syndicate would be well advised to make some independent effort to keep in touch with the progress of the investment. That will mean occasional queries to find out how the property is faring, whether operating expenses are being kept in line, and whether any unanticipated problems have cropped up. The investor, in other words, must not hand money over to the syndicate and then just forget about it. For example, I know of all too many cases where investors, expecting a certain tax write-off, are shocked at year's end to discover that the anticipated benefits have been reduced substantially because of "unforeseen circumstances."

The investor's vigilance, while sound business practice, can, on occasion, prove to be of critical importance. I know of one investor, also a doctor, who had his accountant *and* attorney review his syndicate investments periodically. In the course of one review, the investor's agents discovered that the syndicator had been diverting funds from his current syndications to keep some of his *past* syndications from collapsing. The doctor, who had invested more than $150,000 with the syndicator, was the first investor to discover the fraudulent activity. He immediately demanded the full return of his capital, plus interest. The syndicator, fearing that the doctor would blow the whistle on him, promptly paid up. Had the doctor not been reviewing his investments, he may have awakened one day to read a newspaper account of the syndicator's downfall and the evaporation of his own $150,000.

Investing with Strangers

There are syndicates organized by three or four friends who want to pool their resources in order to exploit the advantages of real estate syndication. When the group is small and the investors all know each other there is, usually, a consensus on what the syndicate's goals should be and how it should be run.

But in most instances, individual investors join huge syndicates where scores, if not hundreds, of people are involved, all perfect strangers to each other. Chances are good that in a large group, a few unreasonable (or unrealistic investors) can create problems. For example, in recent years there has been a movement to "democratize" syndications, to take some discretionary powers away from the syndicators and put those powers in the hands of the investors. While the move was meant to give investors some say in the way their funds are handled, democratization has also given rise to sometime bitter conflicts within the syndicate groups. Votes in democratic groups are apportioned according to the contributions made by each investor. Thus, two or three investors who have contributed more than 50 percent of the capital can ram through decisions affecting the circumstances under which the commonly held property is resold—even if there are a dozen other investors involved who have opposing ideas. Even if the syndicate does not break into two groups, one dominant and one powerless, there is room for trouble. When no one investor or group of investors gains the upper hand, prolonged bickering and infighting can mean that a potentially favorable sale is lost and that the property may have to be sold later at a lower price.

At the risk of being undemocratic, I feel that it is better for the syndicator to have complete control over the property involved. But, the investor who seeks a syndicate in which individual contributors cannot hold sway must take care to find a syndicator who is competent and reputable, and who is known to act in the best interests of the entire group.

Lack of Liquidity

Virtually any real estate investment will give rise to liquidity problems. After all, a home, a small office building or a six-unit apartment house cannot be sold overnight—even in the hottest of real estate markets.

Liquidity problems, however, are compounded in a syndication. Whether the investor joins a "democratic" syndicate or one in which the syndicator alone is king, the investor has little or no say about the time at which the property is sold. In short, that means that the investor who suddenly faces a cash crisis cannot trade on the property held.

Furthermore, the investor who seeks to raise cash by selling off or transferring his or her syndicate interest will run into a tangle of red tape. Most syndicates are organized as limited partnerships. Federal tax requirements, not to mention state and federal securities regulations, restrict the sale of an interest in a syndicate. Furthermore, the person who wants to buy the investor's limited partnership share has to be approved by the syndicator. Sometimes, the original investors must be given the opportunity to purchase the interest. Finally, in many state-regulated syndications, even if the syndicator approves the sale of the investor's interest, consent to the transfer of the interest must be given by the state agency that regulates syndicates.

Finally, the legal and regulatory restrictions to the transfer of a syndicate share often take second place to a more important consideration. The main tax benefits of a syndicate investment are usually returned within the first several years of the investment. After that, the benefits decrease substantially. Therefore, if an investor faces a liquidity crisis four or five years after the syndicate was formed, little financial incentive can be offered to spur someone else to pick up the investor's interest. Nothing less than a substantial discount on the price of the share is likely to elicit any interest.

Some syndicators have tried to minimize liquidity problems for their investors by including "buy-back" provisions in the syndicate agreements. But, as might be expected, these often carry restrictions and do not really solve the problem. The best that can be said is that syndicate investments are only for people who can do without their capital for protracted periods of time.

A Word about the Syndication Process

The syndication process is a highly dynamic one. Within very definite time constraints a syndicator must carry out several key steps almost simultaneously:

1. Find a suitable property. Tie it up with an escrow deposit or purchase option. Obtain a loan to finance the purchase.
2. Organize and structure the syndicate partnership.
3. Raise the necessary capital from investors to consummate the purchase.

The extent and nature of the risks inherent in this process—as well as the potential for benefits—will vary from syndicate to syndicate. Hopefully, this book will help you to detect, analyze, and minimize the risks; to evaluate the benefits; and to come to an intelligent investment decision.

2

Types and Structures of Real Estate Syndicate Investments—Risks and Benefits

TYPES OF SYNDICATED INVESTMENTS

If you are leaning toward an investment in real estate through syndication, you have to determine how much money you want to invest, what goals you want to achieve by making your investment, and what risks you are prepared to take in order to gain your goals.

Because you must make these basic decisions early and because the array of syndications—covering everything from conventional apartment buildings to federally funded housing projects—can be dazzling, it is worthwhile examining the more common opportunities available to you and the significant benefits and risks inherent in each one.

Apartment Buildings

Within the last few years, soaring construction costs and high-interest rates on real estate loans have seriously impeded the construction of new apartment buildings. As a result, existing buildings, particularly those that are well managed, have been able to command high rents while maintaining low vacancy rates. Thus, syndicates that have specialized in buying existing apartment buildings for the most part have been able to return good cash flow, tax benefits, and appreciation profits to their investors while minimizing the risk to the invested capital.

That is not to say that you should consider investing, with unbounded optimism, in apartment building syndications. Because the housing shortage has led to higher rents, apartment buildings have been selling for sums that have astounded and pleased even the most sanguine real estate experts. However, the high prices are based, it must be said, on a somewhat tenuous assumption; namely, that rents will continue to increase at an unabated rate thereby enabling buyers to use the additional revenues to cover increased mortgage and operating costs. But, historically, the American housing market moves through cyclical patterns. One year's housing shortage becomes next year's housing surplus. Moreover, as rents continue to go up, the specter of rent control rises again and again in urban areas across the country. In California, which is generally regarded as the bellwether for trends that will ultimately sweep the nation, rent control proposals elicit increasingly serious consideration, at least on the part of the public.

Anyone interested in apartment building syndicates, therefore, must consider the possibility that natural market forces and/or governmental fiats could depress apartment rents (at least on a short-term basis). If a syndicate were to buy an apartment building at an inflated price and were then stymied in efforts to raise rents sufficiently to cover operating costs, its—and your—investment could very well be compromised.

Shopping Centers

As urbanization continues its spread into the countryside, shopping centers, mushroomlike, crop up virtually overnight in lots, corners, and fields not devoted to yet another housing subdivision. And, while homes and apartments may change hands at a rapid rate, the individual stores within a center are usually let on long-term leases to tenants with sound, if not excellent, credit records. The investor who joins a syndicate looking to buy or develop a shopping center, will run a relatively moderate risk.

But shopping centers do suffer some disadvantages that may discourage you as an investor. They do not provide tax benefits that are as large as those generated by other properties. In the case of shopping centers, a substantial part of the purchase price represents the cost of land—and land cannot be depreciated for tax purposes. And, because leases for major stores are written for long periods of time but with few of the provisions for increasing rent to keep pace with inflation, neither the value of the shopping center nor the profits it returns will increase as sharply or as quickly as those of other potential real estate investments. Thus, a shopping center syndicate may be for you only if you are willing to live with a modest cash return and moderate appreciation in exchange for the assurance that you have made a relatively stable investment.

Office Buildings

Because the tenants who populate an office building can deduct their rent as business expenses, they are usually willing to pay considerably more for their space than people who rent apartments. This means that high cash returns are possible and that the syndicate can offer you substantial returns on your capital. (This, of course, is in addition to standard tax benefits.)

Office buildings, however, usually demand considerable maintenance and steady repairs. They also require continuous and high outlays for utilities and management. Unless you make certain that the syndicator is experienced in office building management and sufficiently sophisticated to write leases that will hedge against the high costs involved, you run the risk that the return on your investment will be lower than you planned.

You should also know that different types of office buildings entail different levels of risk: Office buildings that have stable, long-term tenants will provide a steady cash flow to the syndicate. Office buildings saddled with numerous tenants on short-term leases are likely to cause problems, especially when the economy goes sour and businesses are forced to close their doors. Newer, more modern, and more stylishly designed office buildings will draw more affluent clients because many businesses and corporations are very image conscious. Older buildings often have a hard time attracting and holding tenants.

Because office buildings can provide you with a high return on your investment, syndicates that specialize in them can be a tremendous lure. But because these investments also can be risky, you should research carefully any office building syndicate you are tempted to join.

Industrial Properties

In recent years, an increasing number of syndications have turned their attention to industrial property; that is, property that holds single- or multitenant industrial buildings, usually housing long-term tenants. The property sought by a syndicate may include older buildings located in a growing business area. Or, the property may be a modern industrial park featuring attractive landscaping, parklike grounds, and, on occasion, even swimming pools or tennis courts.

Industrial sites can provide many of the same benefits yielded by other commercial properties. However, industrial properties can be risky because space vacated by one tenant is often hard to rerent, especially in areas where industrial buildings have proliferated. Before investing in an industrial syndicate, make sure that the property is well located, that there is a sufficient demand for space there, and that existing leases have been signed by stable tenants for long, or relatively long, periods of time.

Raw Land Investments

The most important thing to be said about raw land investments is that they are highly risky. Because the property has no revenue-bearing improvements, you, as an investor, will be asked to make additional contributions every year to cover the carrying costs—mortgage payments and taxes—of the property. This risk is magnified for you because the success of the entire investment is often directly dependent on the ability of your coinvestors to contribute the additional cash when the syndicator calls for it. If some of the other investors are financially unable to advance more money when it is needed or if they refuse to increase their investment, the financial burden on you and on those investors who are able and willing to continue will be increased significantly. Moreover, if you and others are willing but not able to bear the greater burden, the property might be lost completely and your investment will be wiped out.

Even if all the investors cooperate at all times in meeting their financial obligations, raw land investments pose considerable risks. Raw land invariably is bought in the hope that it will increase in value with development in the future. But zoning problems, governmental restrictions, battles over environmental impact, recessions and depressions, not to mention erroneous projections, may delay, if not kill, development.

Obviously, there is another side to the coin. Because of the higher risks involved, the return on raw land investment may be far higher than the return on investments in properties already generating income.

In sum, raw land investment is strictly for the gambling investor.

Citrus and Agricultural Properties

An increasing number of syndicators are offering investors the opportunity to become part owners of citrus groves. Three benefits are cited as inducements: (1) The fruit-bearing trees on the property can be depreciated, thereby creating tax deductions for the investor. (2) In time, the land may appreciate in value because it is likely to be developed for commercial or residential purposes. (3) And, in the meantime, income earned by the sale of crops will reduce—if not eliminate altogether—the carrying cost of the property.

Some citrus grove syndications, it must be said, have fulfilled their promise. But others have not lived up to expectations or have failed. The vagaries of the marketplace and the capriciousness of the weather make farming a very chancy business. Even under the most favorable circumstances, many syndicate investors have found that the expense of fertilizing, watering, picking, and marketing all too often exceed by a wide margin the revenues brought by the fruit products. To boot, the risk is great that the farmland will remain farmland, that anticipated development will fail to materialize. In that case, the value of the land will tumble. Finally, faced by the prospect that the farm will not yield either expected profits or capital gains, some of your fellow investors may decide to default on their commitments rather than sink additional monies to meet year-in, year-out carrying costs.

New Construction Properties

Like others of the more glamorous real estate syndicate offerings, investment in construction of new properties can bring a mixed bag of risks and benefits.

You may be attracted to a syndicate about to launch a new building project because the venture offers the opportunity to "get in on the ground floor" and therefore the promise of a sizable profit when the project is finished, rented, or eventually sold. Because many of the costs incurred during construction are tax deductible (costs such as construction loan fees and interest, and property taxes[1]), you stand to reap a good tax write-off (and an even better one if your syndicate decides to use accelerated depreciation allowances).

The concomitant risks, however, can be just as great. Although everyone connected with a new construction project initially is convinced that it will be finished by a promised date and within an outlined budget, it is the rare building that fulfills the optmistic predictions. Bad weather, labor strikes, shortages of materials, and increases in the prices of materials almost always guarantee that a project will be bedeviled by cost overruns—overruns that may have to be financed by the syndicate's investors.

Financing too can be a problem. In order to get a project going, the syndicator will negotiate for a short-term construction loan from a commercial bank. As the apartment building, office complex, or shopping center nears completion, the syndicator will start to shop for a "permanent" or long-term loan from a savings and loan institution or an insurance company to pay back the short-term loan obtained earlier. But often, long-term lenders will not commit themselves to financing the project until they are satisfied that it is viable. If the deadline for paying back the short-term loan arrives before a permanent

---

[1] See Chapter 9 for a discussion on new tax laws affecting some of these deductions.

arrangement has been made, the syndicator, to keep the project going, may be forced to settle for a permanent loan that bears unattractive terms. That is, the new lender may agree to a loan, but at a higher than current interest rate. Or, the lender may offer less money than the syndicator needs. In that case, the investors may find themselves under pressure to advance more money. It is also possible that the syndicator's efforts to find permanent financing may end in complete failure. There, the commercial bank may even foreclose on the project.

Even if all the initial obstacles are conquered, two risks lurk in the background: major expenses like property taxes may have been underestimated or rental rates in the new building may not be as high as expected. Either (or both) circumstance will mean lower cash returns on your investment.

Like raw land development, new construction investments, because they offer potential for high return and because they are riskier, are best suited for the investor who can afford (and, doesn't mind) to take chances.

Rehabilitation of Older Properties

Some syndicators specialize in refurbishing and renovating older properties such as apartment buildings, office complexes, and shopping centers.

Typically, the syndicator will select a mismanaged property which has not been well maintained and which, as a result, has a high number of vacancies and below market rents. He will then modernize the property to make it attractive and competitive. Naturally, he will also attempt to obtain higher rents from current tenants when their leases expire and from new tenants who move into the now more attractive property.

The potential rewards in these syndications can be substantial, especially if the syndicator has the skill and experience to do the job right. If he does, cash flow increases and the value of the property begins to climb.

Of course, if the syndicator miscalculates the cost of the rehabilitation project or is wrong about the building's ability to draw tenants at higher rental rates after rehabilitation, the syndicate may have to settle for a smaller return on its investment, or even a total loss of capital.

Federal Assistance Properties

There are even syndicators who deal in apartment buildings which are funded and financed under a variety of federal programs designed for poor families and the elderly. These programs are administered by the Department of Housing and Urban Development (HUD) through the Federal Housing Administration (FHA). Investors in such syndicates must still contribute capital toward the purchase of a federally subsidized project. However, the government does its share to make the property financially viable by providing mortgage loan insurance, assistance with mortgage interest payments, and rent subsidies for the people who live in the buildings.

Syndicated real estate sustained with the help of federal monies has certain advantages. These projects usually rent for substantially less than prevailing market rents. Thus, they have certain advantages over conventional apartment buildings. Even during high vacancy periods, subsidized housing is likely to be almost full. These real estate ventures, through favorable tax laws, also offer significant tax advantages.[2]

There are, as might be expected, drawbacks. The HUD projects are subject to considerable governmental restrictions and supervision. Prospective tenants are primarily families with low average annual incomes, and to remain eligible for subsidies, their income may not exceed prescribed levels established by the FHA. In addition, rentals must be calculated so that they do not exceed a 6 percent cash return on your invested capital. Further, rental increases cannot be implemented without specific FHA approval. Also to be reckoned with is the fact that these investments typically require substantial repairs and maintenance expenditures that can cut back even further (more than 6 percent) on the cash return on your investment. Finally, there are restrictions on the subsequent sale and refinancing of these projects that can significantly affect the value and marketability of the investment. For example, a HUD project cannot be sold without FHA approval until the 20th year of operations. Also, since the unit sizes of these properties are small, they are not suitable for later conversion to conven-

---

[2] See Chapter 9 for a discussion of the tax aspects of these investments.

tional housing. Consequently, there are few prospective purchasers for these properties.

If the project ultimately fails, as many do, you will not only lose your capital investment, but you will also be required to report as taxable income all the previous tax deductions you received from the investment.

If, despite all these warnings, you are still thinking of investing in a syndicate offering federal assistance property, make sure that the property is well located, that the syndicator is a good property manager and has experience managing low-cost housing, that the syndicator has set aside reserves for contingencies (in addition to those required by FHA regulations), and, if possible, that the syndicator will give you some secured guarantee against a negative cash flow or operating deficits. Finally, try to get the syndicator to take most of the syndication fee in the form of an equity interest in the property, rather than a front-end cash fee. These investments, more than conventional investments, require a conscientious syndicator, and this should provide additional incentive to the syndicator.

SYNDICATE STRUCTURES

Public Syndications

Under federal and most state securities statutes, real estate syndicate investment interests (as they are more formally known) are considered to be securities offerings. That means that the syndicator must register with the appropriate agencies —and gain their approval—before offering or selling interests in the venture to investors, unless certain exemptions are present.

For example, the federal registration statute covers syndicates that cross state lines by offering interests to investors in more than one state. But in 1974 the Securities and Exchange Commission (SEC) adopted Rule 146, which exempts interstate syndicates from federal registration if they have no more than 35 investors and if the syndicator has reasonable grounds for believing that potential investors have sufficient knowledge and experience in real estate syndicate investments, or that the investors are represented by a person who has the requisite knowledge and experience, and that the investors can bear the economic risks of the investment.

Finally, Rule 146 provides that the investors must be provided with, and have access to, the same kind of information that would normally be required if the syndication offering were formally registered with the SEC.

Recently, the SEC also came out with Rule 240 which provides an exemption from federal registration to syndicators who do not raise more than $100,000 within a 12-month period, and who do not have more than 100 investors in all of their syndications. This exemption will be most beneficial to small, part-time syndicators.

There is also an exemption from federal registration if the syndicate offering is "intrastate" in nature, or is only offered and sold to investors within one state.

By and large, the various governmental agencies strive to keep syndications under stringent control. They outline how a syndicate must be structured and what fees the syndicator can charge. They guarantee the investors the right to vote to remove the syndicator and to approve the sale of the property. Many state regulatory agencies also try to ensure that a no-man's-land is created between the syndicator's and the investors' interest—to make sure, in other words, that potential conflicts of interest are either minimized or avoided.

For example, sometimes a syndicator is tempted to form a second syndicate to buy the property held by the first syndicate he organized. Obviously in a case like this, the investors in neither syndicate would have guarantees that the syndicator has their best interests in mind.

Of greatest import, every regulatory agency usually has one overriding goal: to make sure that the syndicator discloses all important investment facts to the people who are interested in buying into the syndicate.

All of this quite clearly means that the investor who is attracted to a publicly registered syndicate will get some minimal protection.

That is not to say, however, that you should be lulled into a sense of false security by the sight of the framed SEC or state regulatory agency permit prominently displayed on the syndicator's wood-paneled wall.

All too often, the regulatory agencies, though full of good intentions, lack the expertise to evaluate the economic integrity of the syndicator's proposed investments. As a matter of fact, most regulatory agencies even make it a point not to make a specific judgment about the economic merits of a syndicate plan. Full disclosure, in short, is not going to assure that you will be making a good investment.

There are also economic disadvantages to a public syndication. The formation of a syndication must be a well-choreographed act. Almost simultaneously, the syndicator must find a suitable property, arrange for its purchase, and find and organize the investors who will make up the syndicate. But, because putting together a publicly registered syndicate entails grappling with governmental agencies, the formation of the group may take months. Thus, if a choice property suddenly becomes available, the syndicator may have to ask the seller for a long escrow to allow time for organizational activities to be completed. While some sellers will agree to take their property off the market while registration of the syndicate goes on, they will do so only in consideration of a higher price, a larger cash down payment, or other terms of sale more favorable to them than to the syndicate.

Your ultimate profit as an investor in a publicly registered syndicate may also be cut down by the registration process costs. The syndicator who seeks governmental approval for an investment plan must run the usual maze of bureaucrats and bureaucratic hurdles; that means hiring lawyers and accountants. It means paying filing fees and, to obtain a verified value of the property, appraisal fees. It means that the syndicator has to pay for printing the brochure (which, of course, is designed to be as attractive and rich-looking as possible) that describes the investment being offered. And, while the syndicator does cover all costs at the beginning, ultimately it is the investor who pays. Once the syndicate is approved and on its way, the syndicator passes all the expenses on to the investors.

Private Syndications

As you might expect, the sundry rules and regulations that call for the registration of syndicates allow for an exception.

A syndicate does not need governmental stamps of approval if it is a "private offering." What exactly is a "private offering?" That depends, in large part, upon the state you live in. But, generally speaking, a private offering means that the investment opportunity has been made available to no more than 25 persons and that the syndicate, when actually formed, includes no more than 10 men and women.

And as you might *also* expect, most syndicators try to come under the private offering umbrella. Not that there is chicanery necessarily involved. But quite obviously, a private offering avoids all the red tape that makes a public syndication an often expensive nightmare. Furthermore, because there are fewer organizational and promotional costs, the syndicator can use more of your dollars (if you invest in a private offering, that is) for the purchase of the real estate and fewer for the syndication process.[3] Because the private syndicate can be organized in short order, it can take advantage of the attractive real estate opportunities that flash only quickly across the investment horizons.

The pitfalls of a private syndicate are self-evident. While a large, publicly registered syndicate can often hire a wide assortment of experts who can help maximize potential profits from a real estate venture, the private syndicate must often rely solely on the wits and abilities of the lone syndicator. While most private syndicators are honest, hardworking people, it is an undeniable truth that the exemption from regulation given private offerings often draws the operator who wants to avoid airing all the facts about the investment being offered. As a result, private syndications—unless you know the organizer to be reputable—do not always offer you the built-in safeguards you have a right to expect.

Blind Pool Syndications

Recently, a new form of public real estate syndication has emerged to compete with the more standard public and private syndicates—the "blind pool" or "public fund" syndicate. These syndicates are organized to invest in a general real estate area (i.e., commercial properties) without committing themselves

[3] Even a private syndication runs up expenses. See Chapter 6.

to a specific property (the Spend-Quick Shopping Center on 4th Avenue and Del Mar, for example) at the time the money is raised.

Blind pool syndications have advantages to recommend them. With money in the bank, the syndicator has time to look around for a good investment opportunity and can move quickly once it is found. The syndicator can offer the seller a short escrow or purchase period and show that money is available to consumate the deal quickly. Faced by the prospect that the property can be sold with minimal or no inconvenience, the seller may be willing to lower the asking price or to accept terms more favorable to the syndicate. And because blind pool syndicates buy multiple properties with their funds, your investment is diversified and cushioned against loss.

As far as you are concerned, there are some disadvantages to the blind pool arrangement. While the syndicate's organizer may have established broad guidelines that outline what kind of real estate will eventually be purchased, no one knows at the beginning the specifics of the properties that will fall into the syndicate's hands. This means that you have no way of assessing the economic soundness of your investment before you write out the check. If you decide to enter this kind of syndicate, therefore, you will have to rely heavily on the knowledge and skill of the syndicator behind the deal. Even if your syndicator ranks high in your estimation, you may find that your money is not working well. It may just sit in a low-interest trust savings account for weeks, or even months, because no attractive piece of property has come on the market or within the grasp of your syndicate. And, you may find that your syndicator, anxious to put the investors' money to use, may finally have to *buy something*. In that case, the syndicator will not be able to negotiate properly or to drive a hard bargain.

CONCLUSION

In this chapter, I have discussed the broad types and structures of real estate syndicates and their investments. Some may present fewer risks than others, but they can all prove to be profitable for you. The type or structure you select will depend on your preferences and financial goals. Therefore, the balance of this book is devoted to information that will help you evaluate specific investments, regardless of type or structure, and minimize your investment risks while maximizing your potential profits.

3

Selecting the Right Syndicator

As an attorney who specializes in real estate law, my practice is kept busy by people who must resort to litigation to salvage the remnants of a bad syndicate investment. More often than not, an initial conversation with a depressed client who has watched thousands of dollars vanish in a real estate venture, will go something along these lines:

"Did you make any inquiries about what you were getting into?"

"Well, sure. Some. You know. I asked where the property was. How much it was worth. What kind of money I would have to come up with. What write-offs I would get. What kind of profit I could expect. That sort of thing."

"Did you ask the syndicator anything about himself?"

The usual reply to this question will be a blank stare. Invariably these are the questions investors never ask the syndicator: "What is your real estate background? What are your qualifications? What kind of properties are you involved with now?"

Perhaps there is an element of naiveté, or embarrassment. After all, it is very difficult, even for the most hardened among us, to look directly at other people and ask them, point blank, to justify themselves in our eyes.

Yet, a thorough investigation of a syndicator is one of the best insurance policies you have against an investment failure. There are thousands of syndicators, hawking tens of thousands of possible syndicate investments. If you are to avoid failure—or, on a more positive level, if you are to assure yourself a good probability of success—you must differentiate among all of the syndicators who are waving enticing brochures at you. You must make sure that the syndicator you ultimately choose is able to negotiate skillfully for an investment property, can take the proper precautions to safeguard your investment, and knows how to minimize the risks inherent in any real estate project. That means you must delve carefully into the syndicator's skill, experience, competence, reputation, and financial resources.

DETERMINING THE SYNDICATOR'S SKILL AND EXPERIENCE

You should start your inquiry at the most basic level; determine if the syndicator has any real estate experience. In a hot real estate market, everyone, from artist to teacher to aerospace engineer, suddenly thinks that he or she can make a quick fortune syndicating property. Thus, is the syndicator you are considering a real estate attorney? A developer? A broker? An accountant?

Naturally, almost any syndicator you approach with these queries will be prepared with a resumé that outlines an unparalleled real estate background. But the resumé's long tribute to the syndicator's experience, credentials, and previous syndications does not lend objective testament to the syndicator's skill and competence.

Your next step, then, should be to establish if the syndicator's previous efforts have been successful. If you use the following checklist, you should be able to make a fairly good analysis:

1. Find out how many other projects the syndicator has organized before.
2. Determine whether the benefits—cash distributions, equity buildup, tax write-offs—promised participants in earlier syndications actually came to fruition. If there was a difference between promised and actual benefits, try to find out why performance did not live up to expectations. If too many of the syndicator's past efforts have fallen short

of their goals, you know that you should look for another syndicator.

3. Determine whether the syndicator's previous projects appreciated in value by comparing purchase and selling prices for each one. If the other projects did not climb in value or climbed only a little, you can conclude that the syndicator paid too much for them or did not manage them properly.
4. Ask the syndicator for a complete list of people who invested in previous projects. The successful syndicator should be more than happy to give you the list because investors who have made money are a valuable asset. In any case, once you have the list, select several investors at random and ask them for their opinion of the syndicator.
5. Ask the syndicator if the Internal Revenue Service has audited any of his past syndications and whether the tax write-offs the syndicator designed passed muster with the IRS. If you find that many of the tax write-offs the syndicator promised investors were not allowed by the Service you will know that the syndicator takes too many risks in structuring tax benefits.
6. Look at other properties the syndicator may be managing currently. Inspect them to see how they are being maintained, what percentage of the apartments, offices, or shops are leased? If other buildings are well managed, you'll know that the syndicator's ability to run a property well will go a long way toward assuring you good cash returns while your syndicate owns a property, and high profits when the project is sold.
7. Try to establish as much as you can through independent investigation. But, if you must rely for some or all information on the syndicator (that is, for data about the number of projects the syndicator has, about the benefits realized in other syndications, about investors in other projects, about IRS treatment of tax write-offs taken in other syndications), make sure that the syndicator puts the facts and figures on paper. An intelligent syndicator will be loath to put false information in black and white because a letter bearing inaccurate information could well give a basis for a later fraud action.

DETERMINING THE SYNDICATOR'S PROFESSIONAL REPUTATION

In your preliminary research to find out all you can about the syndicator, you turned to some previous investors to get a reading on his (or her) previous successes.

Your inquest should not stop there. Because the syndicator you ultimately select is a person in whom you must have complete—almost blind—confidence later, because the syndicator will be handling *your* money, and because the syndicator will be responsible for your money's growth, you must be absolutely sure that you have selected someone of unimpeachable honesty and integrity.

In addition to the syndicator's past investors, you should check with the following:

1. Financial institutions such as commercial banks or savings and loan institutions that have dealt with the syndicator.
2. Real estate boards—especially if the syndicator is a real estate broker or claims extensive contacts in the real estate community.
3. Any professional organizations or clubs in which the syndicator claims membership.

You really should:

1. Try to get to know the syndicator personally and put yourself in a position where you can assess the syndicator's character first hand.
2. Deal with the syndicator directly. Many syndicators surround themselves with batteries of agents or sales personnel. I would say that your initial contacts with these people should be limited to the procedural or minor aspects of the syndicate. The important questions should be taken up only with the syndicator. If you get a runaround about appointments or meetings, or get a hurried interview when you do sit down together, look elsewhere for an outlet for your money.

FINANCIAL RESOURCES OF THE SYNDICATOR

At this time I will review a case describing the financial resources of the syndicator.

In the early 1970s, a syndicate group with which I am familiar bought an apartment building in a growing, expensive area in the San Fernando Valley. There were some problems with the building, but after two years, the project had reached the break-even point.

Just as the syndicators were beginning to mull over the property's future, expensive new condominiums started to mushroom in the vicinity of the syndicate's apartment building. It didn't take long for the syndicators to realize that there was a strong demand for condominiums, that they were selling almost as fast as they were being completed.

While their apartment building would in time prove to be a profit-making venture, the syndicators decided its profitability could be hastened and increased if the individual apartments were converted into condominiums and then sold. The process, though, would be costly. But rather than go back to their investors for additional funds, the syndicators personally advanced $300,000 to finance the necessary conversions and improvements that would make their apartments attractive as condominiums.

Because the apartment building had been erected at a time when construction costs were far lower than they were when the newer condominiums were being built, the syndicators were able to sell their converted apartment units at half the price for which the competitive condominiums were being offered. After eight months, the syndicators' investors received the full return of their original capital, plus an additional 80 percent profit.

A syndicator who has sound financial resources, in other words, can be of great value to you. Skill, experience, and integrity notwithstanding, it is the syndicator's fiscal stability that will lend credence to whatever promises or guarantees come your way. A healthy bank account will support the syndicator's ability and willingness to stay with the project should the going get rough.

The depth and breadth of the syndicator's resources are also important because they act as deterrents to marginal investments. The syndicator who does not have to worry about the next meal, who does not look upon your particular syndicate as the sole source of income, can be more prudent, take some time, and look around for a choice property to buy. A financially stable syndicator will also be able to establish—and stick to—restrictive guidelines and conditions that should prevail when a property is chosen for purchase. The syndicator with good finances is in a position to deal effectively with investors who are disgruntled even though the investment is a good one. Many successful investments have been soured by one, or a few, dissatisfied investors. If the syndicator is in a position to buy them out, which is often the best and only solution to the grumbling, your long-range interests are protected.

Finally, if the syndicator has resources, chances are good that property management, which often depends on the syndicator's checkbook, will be sound and that the building will keep its tenant roster full or nearly full.

There is, in short, no way of overemphasizing the importance of the syndicator's financial standing. All the promises in the world about high tax write-offs, high returns on your investment, and good cash flow will come to naught if the syndicator does not have the means to secure and protect the syndicate's investment.

This means that you should always review and analyze the syndicator's financial statements and references before joining a syndicate. In fact, even if one investment with a syndicator has proven profitable, you should, nevertheless, repeat your financial scrutiny if you make another investment with the syndicator. Real estate is a volatile business, and a syndicator's financial fortunes can change dramatically within a short time.

Following are the steps you can take to assure yourself of the syndicator's financial health:

1. If possible, obtain a financial statement that is the result of an independently conducted audit of the syndicator's current financial standing. If the syndicator does not have an audited statement, ask him (or her) to provide you, at the very least, with the last financial statement he prepared for a bank. The statement should also include facts and figures on corporations or business entities in which the syndicator has controlling interest.

2. Obtain and analyze an independently prepared profit and loss statement for the last few years. Better yet, obtain copies of the syndicator's tax returns (if the syndicator will

release them) for the immediate past. The syndicator's financial statement may be rosy and show a high net worth; but the syndicator's business may have fallen off considerably. For example, the syndicator's balance sheet may show a net worth of $1.5 million. But that in essence is a static figure. The syndicator's profit and loss statement, on the other hand, may show losses of $200,000 annually for the last two years; a more dynamic indication of the trends in the syndicator's current dealings.

3. Look at the financial statements to make sure that the syndicator's liquidity is adequate. Many syndicators show that they have substantial net worth. But that may be based on equity in other real estate projects. You are more interested in cash or cash equivalents such as stocks or bonds the syndicator has on hand because that, more than anything else, will control the syndicator's ability to perform properly.

4. Check carefully to determine whether the values attributed to the syndicator's major assets are reasonable. Find out whether any of those assets are pledged as collateral for the performance of other, major obligations.

5. Find out where the syndicator banks. Check with the bank's officers to determine the syndicator's credit rating. Be sure to let the officers know that you are considering making an investment with the syndicator, and that you are relying on their evaluation to help you make a decision.

6. Obtain a list of the financial institutions that have made real estate loans for the syndicator's projects. Contact those lenders and ask if the syndicator makes mortgage payments on time, whether the syndicator has defaulted on any loans, and whether foreclosure action has ever been taken against any of the syndicator's projects.

7. Find out what the syndicator's liabilities are to investors in other syndicates. For example, find out whether the syndicator is guaranteeing certain benefits to those who are participating in other syndications and whether or not any of the syndicator's own assets have been pledged as security for those guarantees. Any contingent liabilities may not show up in the financial statements given you. You should ask the syndicator directly.

8. Check whether the syndicator is involved in any law-

suits. Have other investors, employees, or other parties found it necessary to sue the syndicator?[1] If there are lawsuits pending, find out what they are about, and, more important, what the adverse consequences would be should the syndicator lose.

I realize that a lot of the material I suggest you study may be difficult to obtain, but if you are willing to take the time and make the effort, you will be at least one step ahead of the game.

SOME GENERAL HINTS ABOUT SELECTING A SYNDICATOR

Look Critically at the Syndicator's Operation

You have been given the name of a syndicator. His offices, you find, are plush—rich wood furniture, modern chairs, and expensive paintings on the walls. There is a buzz of high-pitched activity. Several aids are talking on the telephone, secretaries are running around, and the syndicator himself is surrounded by a group of men and women with whom he is conferring.

Don't be overly impressed. The syndicator who is running a large-scale operation may need all that office space and the large staff to cope adequately with the demands of a seemingly successful business. But real estate syndication is more unstable than most businesses. It ebbs and flows, rides high, and sinks low in unpredictable fluctuations and cycles. When the real estate market goes flat or when money markets tighten, the syndicator who has to make high rent and salary payments may be tempted to undertake syndication ventures that involve a large risk component, just because money is needed to cover the now burdensome overhead expenses.

A large-scale syndicator may prove beneficial to you. But make sure it is a man or woman who can afford to wait out hard times and who does not have to form investment groups just to stay in business. Often you will be better off with syn-

---

[1] The syndicator may tell you about the lawsuits if you ask. If the syndicator does not and you have any suspicions, spend a couple of hours with court records to satisfy your curiosity. Courts keep lists of all defendants and plaintiffs involved in litigation and you can run through the lists to see if your syndicator is scheduled for a day in court. The lists will also give you information you need to find the court files about the case.

dicators who keep a low profile and a low overhead such as an accountant, a lawyer, a real estate broker, or any expert in real estate who also has a source of income other than syndication. Find a syndicator who can earn a living elsewhere and you'll find someone who can afford to be more selective in buying properties for syndication (and will, therefore, give your investment added security) and someone whose low overhead expenses will keep a lid on syndication costs, thereby increasing the overall return on your investment.

Ask: Who Pays for the Band?

All too often, syndicators will spare little in their efforts to lure you into their fold. They will prepare elaborate brochures full of charts, statistics, and fine photography. They'll sponsor seminars and hold lectures, all with one aim in mind; that is, to explain just how good an investment opportunity they are making available. But as you collect the pamphlets and sit through the seminars, ask yourself one question: "Who is paying for all of this?"

Then answer yourself: "I am."

In time, all the costs the syndicator has incurred in forming the syndicate will find their way into the syndication fees charged to the investors. And that means smaller profits for you.

Find out if the Syndicator Has Faith in Himself

As a general rule, you should not invest with a syndicator who does not have a direct, continuing financial interest in the syndicate. A syndicator should have enough confidence in a project to invest personal funds, or to accept a substantial portion of the syndication fee in the form of a profit or equity interest in the syndication.[2] The syndicator who has a financial interest in the syndication will be more motivated and conscientious in managing and supervising your investment.

I realize that the criteria outlined in this chapter can work against entrepreneurs who are syndicating their first properties. However, while newly minted syndicators may have con-

---

[2] Syndication fees are discussed further in Chapter 4.

siderable abilities, you should think twice before investing with someone who is untried. The risks are just too great. But if you select a syndicator who meets the qualifications discussed above, you should be well on your way toward a profitable syndicate investment.

4

The Syndicator's Fee—Is It Fair?

Probably no other subject in the field of real estate syndication raises as much emotional fervor as the topic of syndicators' fees. Talk to a group of syndicators about a specific piece of property and you'll get businesslike colloquium about its debt service ratio. Ask about tax write-offs and you'll get enough dispassionate information to fill a manual. But question the compensation to which a syndicator is entitled and you'll be lucky to leave the room alive.

Understandably enough. To talk about fees is to talk about the syndicators' personal income, the focal point of their existence. And, before I delve into the darker aspects of the subject, I must stress one important point. You must be able to accept the fact that syndicators are entitled to reasonable compensation for the services they render. After all, it is only fair. A syndicator must spend considerable time and effort searching for investment properties, studying market conditions, negotiating for the purchase of investment properties, and raising the required capital from investors to buy the property.

Adequate compensation must be made because the syndicator is willing to incur substantial financial risks. The syndicator, after all, must pay money into escrow to hold a property until the syndicate is formed. The money might be lost if enough investor capital is not then forthcoming to buy the property. Syndicators, large and small, have overhead expenses that must be covered.

Having said that, let me add that some syndicators do abuse the right to fair and proper compensation by loading excessive and unreasonable fees onto the shoulders of their investors. This chapter, therefore, is meant to help you detect fee arrangements that are excessive in relation to the risks taken and work performed by the syndicator. First, we will examine the more common types of syndication fees. Then, we will evaluate the way many syndicators actually build their fees to an actual investment situation. Finally, you will learn how to detect hidden or disguised syndication fees. If you can do that, you'll be able to come to a more intelligent assessment of the impact of the fee and the way it adds to the real cost of your investment.

TYPES OF SYNDICATION FEES

Front-End Fees

The most prevalent syndication fee is the so-called front-end fee, which is a cash fee paid directly from the initial capital contributions of the investors. Typical front-end fees collected by the syndicator include real estate commissions, finder's fees, and acquisition fees. As we'll see shortly, they can also be disguised as interest, loan fees, consulting fees, or prepaid management fees.

The front-end fee is popular because the syndicator receives the cash in advance. But a front-end fee, if excessive, can create considerable risks for you as an investor. Cash in hand means that the syndicator has less incentive to pay conscientious attention to the project during the time the syndicate owns it. Should anything go wrong, the syndicator, fee already pocketed, may make little or no effort to salvage the investment. Just as important, if a part of the fee is not made contingent on the profit returned at the end of the investment period when the property is sold, the syndicator will have virtually no incentive to select a piece of property that is advantageously priced, to manage it well so that its value increases as much as possible, or to obtain the best price and terms when new buyers come along.

Front-end fees, especially if they are high, can seriously affect the return on your investment. For example, let's assume that the purchase price of an apartment building bought by your syndicate is $1 million. The syndicator collects $200,000 from you and your fellow investors. Since the syndicate agreed to a 6 percent front-end sales commission, the syndicator banks $60,000 (6 percent of $1 million) and uses the rest of the invested capital ($140,000) to make the down payment on the building.

Under a more favorable (to you) fee arrangement, the syndicator would have used the full $200,000 as a down payment. But in this case, only 70 percent of the capital is actually applied to the purchase of the property. Thus, there is an immediate 30 percent dilution in invested capital. This will mean a 30 percent reduction on the return on your investment. It will mean a domino effect that will affect the very security and safety of the investment: A $140,000 down payment creates a larger debt service on the property because a larger loan ($860,000 as opposed to $800,000) must be obtained to cover the purchase price. A higher debt service means a higher break-even point. To reach that break-even point, the syndicator may have to raise rents and price the property out of the market. Some tenants may move out. Fewer prospective tenants may be drawn to the property. Cash returns diminish. You can see where the scenario can lead.

Because excessive front-end fees can pose a danger, many state regulatory agencies restrict the up-front monies that can be drawn by syndicators who run public syndications. In California, for example, the organizer of a syndicate with more than 100 investors cannot ask for a front-end fee that exceeds 18 percent of *invested capital;* that is, syndicators in these large investment groups can no longer charge a percentage of the purchase price of the property. The new rules are meant to ensure that most of the investors' money will go to its intended target, the real estate being purchased.

The regulations will also discourage high leverage investments. Large syndicators, in order to keep their up-front earnings high, will be required to raise larger sums of money to use as invested capital. By collecting more capital and by using it to make larger down payments, the syndicator will be creating greater equity in the investment thereby increasing its security.

I must emphasize that I am not opposed entirely to front-end fees. Syndicators, no matter how modestly they run their operations, do have recurring overhead business expenses. And, of course, they have personal living expenses. Thus, they are entitled to some front-end compensation.

Still, I must also stress that you should make sure that the front-end fee will be reasonable and that it will only be a part of the syndicator's total fee. In other words, the greater portion of the syndicator's compensation should come later, when the investment venture comes to an end. Thus, the syndicator will have an incentive to do a good job, day to day, month to month, until the syndicate has reached its investment goals. The conscientious and honest syndicator, who plans to offer you other properties for investment, will gladly accept this kind of a fee arrangement. After all, he wants to make sure that you are satisfied and, therefore, willing to reinvest when other syndications come along.

Straight Participation Fees

Many syndicators, aware of the objections to full front-end compensation, will take all or part of their fees in the form of an equity or ownership interest in the property.

This form of participation, or "taking a piece of the action," also has a diluting effect on your invested capital and on the rate of return you can expect. Nevertheless, under this fee arrangement, a large portion of your money can still be earmarked for use in buying the property. As we discussed before, the greater the amount of capital that can be applied to the purchase of the property, the greater the equity, the smaller the debt service, and, therefore, the greater the safety of the investment.

Of course, compensation based on participation meets many of the objections to the front-end fees. Because a participation fee confers equity interest, it serves to keep the syndicator interested in the investment. The syndicator will undoubtedly have the stimulus to do all that is possible to make the investment a good one and to make it as profitable as possible.

A fee arrangement that gives the syndicator an equity share in the property can also pose risks to you. You must make sure that the equity share is to be paid only if the property is sold at a price that will—at the very least—recoup your original investment, or is to be paid after a period of time that gives the property a reasonable chance to increase in value sufficiently to return a profit to you and to cover the syndicator's fee. If some limitations are not written into the partnership agreement and the syndicator is unscrupulous, you could still lose mightily, despite the alleged safeguards of the participation fee structure. For example, let's assume that the $1 million property mentioned earlier was bought with a $200,000 down payment but with the provision that the syndicator would receive a 20 percent equity share in the property. Without proper restrictions, the syndicator could simply turn around and resell the property for the same price as bought, $1 million. You and your fellow syndicators would make nothing. But the syndicator would earn a healthy $40,000 (20 percent of the $200,000 equity in the property). In fact, you would even lose on the deal because the net proceeds of the sale would only be $960,000. The syndicator would get $40,000, the bank $800,000, and you and your fellow investors $160,000—less than you contributed.

Operational Fees

Many syndicators take compensation in the form of payments for managing the property. This type of fee, called an operational fee, is usually based on a percentage of gross revenues on the investment property. It is often in addition to other fees (i.e., equity fee or front-end payment) the syndicator may take. Operational fees are justified because the syndicator provides management services during the investment period. Operational fees, however, reduce cash flow to the investors. Furthermore, they provide little financial incentive to the syndicator unless the agreement on compensation provides that the operational fees will be paid only after the investors have received a certain specified cash return. For example, rather than give the syndicator the right to collect 5 percent of gross rental income as a management fee, the compensation schedule, for example, may call for the investors to receive the first 6 percent of cash available from operations. Additional amounts may then be divided equally between the syndicator and the investors. Whatever formula is used, it should include ample incentive for the syndicator.

Back-End Fees

A back-end fee is a payment the syndicator receives when the property is sold. It usually is made before the proceeds of the sale are distributed to the investors. The back-end fee comes about because many syndicators hold real estate licenses. Thus, they can list their own syndicated properties and receive a listing fee or sell it and receive a sales commission on the sale. A back-end fee, of course, reduces the net proceeds available for the investors. If the syndicate you are interested in calls for a back-end fee for the syndicator, make sure that it will be paid only after the investors have been refunded their capital contributions and have been paid a fair return on their investment. A provision that calls for payment of a back-end fee only after the investors have been satisfied will spur the syndicator to obtain a higher sales price for the property.

Subordinated Profit Fees

In researching syndicate investments, you may also run into the subordinated profit fee. One version of the subordinated fee arrangement allows the syndicator to receive a percentage of the profits generated by the sale of the investment, but only after the investors have been given back their original capital. Whatever profits remain are shared between syndicator and the group of investors according to a predetermined formula—say, 20 percent to syndicator, 80 percent to investors. Thus, let's assume that in the hypothetical case mentioned earlier, the property is sold for $1.1 million. First, the investors would get the $200,000 in capital they advanced for purchase of the property. Then, they would collect $80,000 (80 percent of the remaining $100,000 in net proceeds) and the syndicator would pocket $20,000.

Another version of the subordinated fee calls for the syndicator to receive a portion of the annual cash flow generated by the investment. Again, the investors must first get their share each year before the syndicator is entitled to participate. After the investors have received a designated portion (say, 8 percent on invested capital), they and the syndicator share the rest.

I personally feel that the subordinated fee system is the fairest form of syndication compensation. The syndicator benefits directly by performance and, as a result, has considerable financial incentive to find a good property, manage it well, and obtain the highest possible resale price when the property is put back on the market. The subordinated fee ensures that the syndicator's interests parallel those of the investor. At the same time, in today's rising real estate market, the subordinate fee can produce even greater profit for the syndicator than the standard front-end fee. And why not? The syndicator, under a subordinate fee arrangement, can produce a profitable investment while safeguarding the capital of the investors.

HOW TO EVALUATE SYNDICATION FEES

It would be nice if there were some simple way for you to determine the "going rate" for syndication fees and to compare the impact of the fees of the various syndicators whose offerings you are considering. Unfortunately, the types and structures of fees vary from one syndication to another, and are not always expressed in straightforward monetary terms. Thus, you are often hard-pressed to make an evaluation. Furthermore, the complexity of judging fees is compounded even further when you consider that the monetary aspects of the syndicator's fees are not the only variables. You also have to weigh what kind of a motivation and incentive the fee structure imposes on the syndicator, and what kind of risks the fee structure imposes on the investment.

To assist you in the evaluation process, let's compare several commonly used fee structures and study them in the context of an actual investment situation. To simplify matters somewhat, the same basic investment is assumed in each case.

The Investment

A 44-unit apartment building located in Cleveland, Ohio, is being purchased by ABC Syndication. The building has a gross annual income of $180,000. The purchase price is $1.3 million and the down payment is $260,000, exclusive of real estate commissions. A new first trust deed (or mortgage) loan of $950,000, with annual principal and interest payments of $90,000, will be obtained by ABC Syndication. The seller will take back a second trust deed of $90,000 payable at $8,000 per year. Annual operational expenses, exclusive of management fees, are estimated to be $68,000.

Fee structure 1. The syndicator will receive a real estate commission from ABC of $78,000 and will, thereafter, manage the apartment building for a fee equal to 5 percent of gross rents. In addition, on the subsequent resale of the property, the syndicator will receive 10 percent of proceeds remaining after the investors of ABC have recouped their initial investment.

Fee structure 2. The syndicator will receive a fee of $25,000 for organizing ABC Syndication and a $25,000 consulting fee for advising ABC during its first year of operation. The syndicator will also manage the apartment building for an annual fee equal to 5 percent of the gross rents. The first year's fee of $9,000 will be paid in advance. In addition, when the property is resold, the syndicator will receive 10 percent of proceeds remaining after the investors of ABC have recouped their initial investment.

Fee structure 3. The syndicator will receive a fee of $10,000 for organizing ABC Syndication and will, thereafter, manage the apartment building for a fee equal to 6 percent of the gross rents. The 6 percent fee will be paid only if the investors have first received an annual cash distribution equivalent to 6 percent on their invested capital. In addition, the syndicator will receive 40 percent of the proceeds remaining after the investors of ABC have recouped their initial investment.

Fee structure 4. The syndicator will receive a real estate commission from ABC of $35,000 and will, thereafter, manage the apartment building for a fee equal to 3 percent of the gross rents. In addition, the syndicator will receive an equity participation interest of 20 percent.

Evaluating the Financial Impact of Fee Structures

In Table 1, structures 1 and 2, you will note, carry substantially higher front-end fees. Thus, if you are considering

TABLE 1
Cash Flow Analysis

	Fee Structure			
	1	*2*	*3*	*4*
Gross annual rents	$180,000	$180,000	$180,000	$180,000
Less:				
First mortgage payments	90,000	90,000	90,000	90,000
Second mortgage payments	8,000	8,000	8,000	8,000
Operating expenses	68,000	68,000	68,000	68,000
Management fee	9,000	9,000	—	5,400
Net cash flow	$ 5,000	$ 5,000	$ 14,000	$ 6,888*
Invested capital†	$338,000	$319,000	$270,000	$295,000
Percent cash return	1.48%	1.56%	5.18%	2.33%

* Actual cash flow is $8,600, but the syndicator is entitled to 20 percent of cash flow, or $1,720, as a 20 percent equity owner.
† Invested capital consists of the $260,000 down payment plus the front-end fees.

only return on investment, they are less desirable than structures 3 and 4. The higher the front-end fee, remember, the lower the cash return on investment. High front-end fees also cut down on returns on investment attributable to tax savings.

Structure 3 initially produces a higher cash return than 4. But that may not be the case in subsequent years. You must keep in mind that the assumed facts apply only to the first year. In most investments, rents increase and, therefore, cash flow increases can reasonably be expected. As more cash comes in, the 6 percent subordinated management fee contained in structure 3 will come into effect. At some point it will actually exceed the 3 percent guaranteed management fee in 4. Thus, the primary difference between structures 3 and 4 is that 3 has a lower down side risk. That is to say, if the property is not generating sufficient cash flow, the syndicator in 3 is affected more than the investors. On the other hand, if the property generates high cash flow, the syndicator in 3 benefits handsomely.

Table 2 shows the downside risk for each fee structure. Obviously, the lower the front-end fee, the lower the break-even point for the property. Thus, structure 3 is once again more favorable to the investor than the other structures.

Structure 4 is interesting because in giving the syndicator a 20 percent full equity participation, it has the highest downside risk. The downside risk could be lessened by putting cer-

TABLE 2
Break-Even Analysis

	Fee Structure			
	1	*2*	*3*	*4*
Purchase price.........	$1,300,000	$1,300,000	$1,300,000	$1,300,000
Front-end fees..........	78,000	59,000	10,000	35,000
Back-end fees..........	—	—	—	73,750
Break-even sales price....	$1,378,000	$1,359,000	$1,310,000	$1,408,750*

* Remember, the syndicator has a 20 percent equity interest. To calulated this amount, you should use the following formula:

C = Original investors' capital ($295,000 in our example, consisting of $260,000 down payment plus $35,000 commission)
X = Amount necessary to recoup C plus syndicator's 20 percent interest
$X = C + 0.20x$
$X = \$295,000 + 0.20x$
$0.80x = \$295,000$
$X = \$368,750$
Syndicator's portion = 20% × $368,750 = 73,750

tain restrictions on the syndicator's interest. For example, you can insist that the syndicator receive an equity share only if the property's resale price exceeds the original cost of purchase. This restriction would make for a subordination of the fee. You could also insist that the syndicator's equity be vested only if the property is sold after a certain period of time after the original purchase, such as three years. That would allow enough time for the property to appreciate in value sufficiently to offset the diluting effect of the syndicator's full equity participation.

Let us now add one variable to our set of assumptions. Let's assume that the property will appreciate an average of 5 percent per year and that the property is sold after four years for 20 percent more, or $1,560,000.

How do the different fee structures affect each of the syndicators and investment groups? Although Syndicator 3 received a small front-end fee, the total fee paid was $110,000, far more than the $96,200 fee Syndicator 1 earned. (See Table 3.) But even though Syndicator 3 earned more than Syndicator 1, the investors in group 3 did not suffer because they received a higher return on their investment than the participants in group 1.

Because the fee structure in group 4 included front-end fees

TABLE 3
Appreciation-in-Value Analysis

	Syndicator			
	1	*2*	*3*	*4*
Sales price	$1,560,000	$1,560,000	$1,560,000	$1,560,000
Less:				
Purchase price.......	1,300,000	1,300,000	1,300,000	1,300,000
Front-end fees........	78,000	59,000	10,000	35,000
Back-end fees........	18,200*	20,100†	100,000‡	97,000§
Profit to investors‖......	$ 163,800	$ 181,100	$ 150,000	$ 128,000
Invested capital........	$ 338,000	$ 319,000	$ 270,000	$ 295,000
Percent return on invested capital.............	48.46%	56.77%	55.5%	43.38%

* Computed $1,560,000 − $1,300,000 − $78,000 = Profit of $182,000 × 0.10 (subordinated fee) = $18,200.

† Computed $1,560,000 − $1,300,000 − $59,000 = Profit of $201,000 × 0.10 (subordinated fee) = $20,100.

‡ Computed $1,560,000 − $1,300,000 − $10,000 = Profit of $250,000 × 0.40 (subordinated fee) = $100,000.

§ Computed $1,560,000 − $1,040,000 (mortgage debt assuming no principal reductions) − $35,000 = Net equity of $485,000 × 0.20 full reductions equity interest = $97,000.

‖ "Profits" as used above is meant in the sense of net proceeds of sale, without taking into consideration the income tax effects of the sale of the property, such as depreciation recapture.

and a full 20 percent equity participation, the syndicator in this instance made more and the investors made less than the principals in the other investment groups.

Table 3 also demonstrates the incentive effect created by subordinated profit fee structures. The substantial back-end fees due Syndicator 3, and to a lesser extent those due Syndicator 4 can be traced to the appreciation in value of each investment. Thus, these syndicators will have considerable incentive to initially select sound investments, and thereafter maximize their values by conscientious management and maintenance.

EVALUATING THE RISK IN VARIOUS FEE STRUCTURES

Structure 1

This fee structure, which includes a real estate commission as a front-end fee, a management fee, and a subordinated fee upon resale of the property, is perhaps the most commonly used in syndication today. It is favored by real estate brokerage companies that have a property management division but whose primary sources of income are commissions earned in buying and selling property. This fee structure is also used by those syndicators who have large staffs and substantial overhead costs.

Fee structure 1 bears a sizable risk for investors. The large front-end fee means that the syndicator will have little financial incentive to do a good job in selecting, managing, and reselling the property. Accordingly, should you decide to invest in a syndicate that has a fee structure like 1, you must take pains to investigate carefully the syndicator's reputation, integrity, and track record (see Chapter 3). In this case, the syndicator's greatest incentive to perform properly will be a personal sense of professional responsibility and investor satisfaction—not just the pure financial reward.

Structure 2

This fee structure, with its up-front organizational and consulting fees, and its management and subordinated fees, is basically the same as fee structure 1. While it also is risky because it provides little incentive to the syndicator, it does have one great advantage: Its fees are low and leave more room for a greater return to the investors.

You should also note that the syndicator has attempted to disguise the nature of some of the fees by calling them "consulting" and "organizational" fees, rather than commissions. Perhaps the syndicator does not have a real estate license and, therefore, cannot accept real estate commissions. There may also be an attempt to deduct the fees on the theory they are ordinary and necessary business expenses, rather than attributable to the cost of acquiring the property. This is particularly risky in light of the Internal Revenue Service's close scrutiny of such tax deductions and the 1976 Tax Reform Act (see Chapter 9). An attempt to deduct such fees could very well trigger an IRS audit. Finally, the syndicator may simply be trying to make the fees more palatable or receptive to the investors by relating them to services rendered.

Structure 3

This fee structure includes a small front-end fee, a management fee payable only after the investors have received a 6 percent return on gross rentals and a subordinated fee upon resale of the property. It is commonly used by "part-time" syndicators such as attorneys, accountants, and other professionals who invest right along with their clients and who do not have high overhead costs.

This fee structure serves the investors well. Because so much of the syndicator's fee is contingent on high returns in the form of rentals while the syndicate holds the investment and in the form of profits when the property is resold, the syndicator has great incentives to perform conscientiously in every aspect of the syndication. Thus, by providing a mutual interest that binds the syndicator to the investors, this fee structure provides a sound margin for investment safety.

Structure 4

Here, the syndicator has elected to take an equity position in the property in lieu of a full commission. The risk is obvious. The syndicator's full equity participation dilutes investment capital by 20 percent. That means the syndicator will profit on the sale of the property even though the investors could lose money. However, as I mentioned earlier, this structure can be modified by making the syndicator's equity participation subordinate to conditions that will eliminate the risks while providing considerable financial incentive for the syndicator to perform conscentiously. Thus 4 can have some of the same merits as 3, without the risks that come with structures 1 and 2.

SOME OTHER CONSIDERATIONS

It is important to remember that, for the sake of giving you some tools for analyzing fee structures, the investment situations outlined above had to be drawn with some very limited and constant factors. Naturally, in the real world, you will have to consider other important factors when you evaluate the fee structures of various syndicate opportunities open to you. Some of the more important additional variables are discussed below.

The Nature of the Investment

Evaluate the fee structure in the context of the type of property that is being syndicated. Some property investments, by their very nature, require more managerial and supervisory time than others. For example, an investment in a property that will require rehabilitation will take more of the syndicator's time than a leaseback investment which does not command much of the syndicator's energy once it has been bought. A fee should be proportional to the time and effort the syndicator must dedicate to the investment.

Investment Guarantees

Some syndicators will guarantee that you will receive a certain cash flow even if the property has a bad year. Other syndicators will write other assurances into the syndication agreement. As you evaluate the syndicator's fee, remember that such guarantees reduce the downside risk of the investment. This safety factor may justify higher fees. (See Chapter 12 about "Investor Guarantees.")

The Skill and Experience of the Syndicator

As we discussed in Chapter 3, the syndicator's skill and experience are extremely important factors when you are looking to make a profitable investment. Thus, if you know the syndicator to be highly competent and if you and the syndicator have had prior dealings, and/or a personal relationship, your evaluation of the syndication fees may take a back seat.

DETECTING HIDDEN SYNDICATION FEES

If you want to analyze and compare syndication fees, you must know the amount and nature of the fees. Unfortunately, some syndicators load their syndications with substantial fees that are almost impossible for the untrained investor to detect. It is important, therefore, that you know how to spot fees that are disguised, not disclosed, or simply too complicated for you to understand, even when the syndicator does put them on the table.

Hidden Real Estate Commissions

Since many syndicators are real estate brokers, they often take the major portion of their syndication fees in the form of large real estate commissions. Although this can be an acceptable practice, some syndicators will either conceal or disguise the fact that they are taking the real estate commissions. Syndicators have one phobia: that an investor who knows what fees are being charged may refuse to join the syndicate.

For example, an offering circular may state, without further comment, that a certain real estate firm will receive a real estate commission from the seller when the syndicate purchases the investment property. If, however, the real estate company is connected with the syndicator, the commission is clearly a syndication fee which the syndicate and you, and not the seller, is paying.

It is even possible that the syndicator will hide two real estate commissions within the same investment transaction. To illustrate, assume the following example. A seller lists his property for $1 million and asks a $200,000 cash down payment. Your syndicator, through his own corporation approaches the seller and offers $1,050,000 with a $250,000 down payment if the seller agrees to pay the syndicator a $50,000 real estate commission. The seller accepts the offer. Your syndicator then forms a limited partnership in which he is the general partner to buy the property from his own corporation for $1.1 million with a $300,000 down payment. When the second sale is consummated, your syndicator is to receive a real estate commission—his second—of $50,000. Your syndicator may not have disclosed to the investors that he has received a real estate commission on each sale. If he does make the disclosure, he may make it appear that the seller actually paid the first commission when, in fact, the investors were the ones to have paid for it. Thus, in the above case, the syndicate pays $100,000 more cash for the property than the original seller would have otherwise received and all of that extra money winds up in the syndicator's pocket.

Many syndicators also do not disclose that they intend to collect a sales or a listing commission when the investment property is resold. In effect, this real estate commission is hidden because the syndicator may want no limitations placed on collecting it. That is, the syndicator may, quite rightly, suspect that the investors may insist that a resale commission should be payable only after they have received a full return on their original capital contributions. In other words, that the commission be subordinate to their interests.

There are several ways in which you can detect hidden real estate commissions. If the investment material mentions nothing about a real estate commission, you should inquire whether a real estate commission is to be paid when the property is bought. If a commission is to be paid, find out who is to receive it and what the recipient's relationship is to the syndicator. Even when there is a disclosure in an offering circular that a real estate commission is being paid, you should ask whether the syndicator or a company with which the syndicator has ties will receive any part of the commission. You should also request certified copies of all escrow instructions and contracts of sale because they will probably contain information about the existence of any real estate commissions. You should make all inquiries and requests to the syndicator by letter. Ask that the requested information also be conveyed in a return letter or other written form. If the syndicator misrepresents the amount or nature of his commission in writing, the syndicator will be liable for misrepresentation or fraud.

Hidden Profits

Some syndicators use the back-to-back sales discussed above to obtain hidden profits as well as real estate commissions. A syndicator may purchase a property with low-interest financing, for example, through a related business entity. Then, the syndicator immediately resells the property to the syndicate with a personal loan made at a higher interest rate.

For example, using an independent corporation, the syndicator buys an investment property for $1 million. The syndicator makes a $200,000 cash down payment and assumes an $800,000 mortgage with an interest rate of 7 percent. The syndicator then resells the property to the syndicate for $1.1 million with a $250,000 down payment. The syndicator then makes a $850,000 loan to the syndicate at an interest rate of 9 percent.

The syndicator "loaned" the syndicate $850,000 at 9 percent interest; that means that the yearly interest payments by the syndicate will be $76,500. However, remember that the syndicator bought the property in the first place with an $800,000 loan at 7 percent interest. Thus, the syndicator, who must pay only $56,000 interest annually makes an additional $20,500 cash profit each year.

To detect such hidden profits, you need to go through a two-step process. First, find out what loan the syndicator obtained to purchase the property in the first place and what interest rate and annual loan payments are involved. Second, compare those figures with the loan payments and interest rate your syndicate is being charged by the syndicator.

Property Management Fees

In some syndications, a portion of the capital raised from the investors will be used to cover "prepaid management fees." The syndicator may tell you these are tax deductible. But they are not. Moreover, when you see a line that says "prepaid management fee," you should immediately suspect that it hides a syndication fee. For example, the syndicator's offering brochure might state that the yearly management fee will be 6 percent of the annual gross income and that the first year's management fee will be prepaid in advance at the close of escrow on December 31, 1979. For the next five years, the offering will also state, the investors will be given a credit for the prepayment. Thus, you will be told, future years' management fees will effectively be only 5 percent of the annual gross income. If gross income remains constant at $200,000 per year, the syndicator will receive a prepaid management fee of $12,000 in December 1979, even though the syndicate did not own the building in that year. The syndicator will also receive a $10,000 management fee for the years 1980, 1981, 1982, 1983, and 1984. Thus, the syndicator will have managed the building for five years, but will have received six management fees.

To determine whether a syndication fee is hidden under the guise of a management fee, you should ask a qualified Realtor or professional property management firm about the going rate for professional management services. In Los Angeles, for example, professional management services run 4 percent to 5 percent of gross income. Thus, in the example above, the syndicate is paying, at the very least, $12,000 for which it receives no real services from the syndicator. After all, the investors are still paying 5 percent per year for management services, even after credit is given for the prepaid management fees. The syndicator has simply overcharged for management services in order to hide an additional syndication fee.

Loan Fees

Syndicators sometimes also hide additional fees by presenting them as substantial loan fees on the sale of a property to the syndicate. However, since the syndicator renders few, if any professional finance services for the syndicate, there is no reason to impose any charges for the loan. Therefore, such charges should be classified as syndication fees and disclosed as such in the offering circular. Accordingly, whenever loan fees are charged to the syndicate, you should inquire who—syndicator? savings and loan institution? mortgage company?—is receiving them, what services are being rendered in exchange for the charge, and the relationship of the party receiving the loan fee to the syndicator.

A portion of an actual offering circular is presented below. See if you can detect hidden fees. Suggestions on how to spot them follow. Use the exercise to improve your ability to detect hidden syndication fees.

REDWOOD VILLAGE APARTMENTS, LTD.

* * * * *

The Offering

The General Partner of REDWOOD VILLAGE APARTMENTS, LTD. (the "Partnership"), ABLE MANAGEMENT, INC. ("Able"), hereby offers to investors an aggregate of

$485,000 of Limited Partnership interests ("Units"), priced at a minimum of $1,000 per unit, with a minimum purchase of 5 units, for the purpose of acquiring an 80-unit apartment complex located in Dallas, Texas. A 7 percent selling commission will be paid on units sold by licensed real estate brokers or licensed broker-dealers. . . .

Acquisition of the Property

ABC PROPERTIES, INC. ("ABC"), a real estate development company, is in the process of acquiring the Property from SAGE CORPORATION ("S") for a purchase price of $1.5 million. ABC's down payment on the Property is $300,000. ABC will accept title to the Property subject to an existing first trust deed, having an unpaid principal balance of $800,000, and bearing interest at 7 percent per annum. The balance of the purchase price will be evidenced by a promissory note to be executed by ABC in the principal amount of $400,000 in favor of S, and bearing interest at 6 percent per annum, interest only, all due and payable at the end of ten years.

The Partnership will then purchase the Property from ABC for $1.6 million, with a down payment of $400,000 and the balance of the purchase price, $1.2 million, to be evidenced by a ten-year promissory note in said amount, bearing interest at 9 percent per annum in favor of ABC, the payment of which promissory note shall be secured by a deed of trust on the Property.

The Partnership will pay $40,000 in loan points to ABC in connection with ABC's making of a loan secured by the Partnership trust deed. The Partnership will also pay Consultants, Inc., a consulting fee in the sum of $7,000 for consulting services designed to improve the net income of the Property. . . .

Application of Proceeds (i.e., Investment Capital Raised).

The $485,000 proceeds from the sale of investment units shall be applied as follows:

Application	*Amount*
1. Down payment	$400,000
2. Loan points	40,000
3. Operating reserves	10,000
4. Selling commissions	28,000
5. Consulting fees	7,000
Total	$485,000

ANALYSIS OF SYNDICATION FEES

1. If you get a circular that does not have an application-of-proceeds section, carefully read the entire offering brochure to determine how all the capital raised from the investors is being used. The amount of total capital raised from investors must equal the total amount applied to the purchase or operation of the property. If there is a discrepancy, you are entitled to assume that syndication fees are hidden in there somewhere.

In this case, the syndicators have included an application-of-proceeds section that makes our job easier. In Redwood Village Apartments \$410,000 of the \$485,000 raised is being applied toward a reduction in the purchase price through a down payment or for operation of the property. To be precise, \$400,000 is earmarked for the down payment, and \$10,000 for the creation of operating reserves. The remaining \$75,000 raised from the syndicate through the sale of investment units represents potential syndication fees.

2. As you analyze the underlying financing of the entire syndication structure, it becomes apparent that ABC will receive yearly interest of \$108,000 (0.09 × \$1.2 million) on the loan to the partnership. From that \$108,000, ABC needs to pay only \$80,000 (0.07 × \$800,000 + 0.06 × \$400,000) to Sage. Thus, ABC makes a profit of \$28,000 per year. Consequently, over the ten-year period of the promissory note, ABC will earn \$280,000. This \$280,000 in excess interest represents a hidden syndication fee.

3. The \$40,000 in loan fees payable to ABC represents a syndication fee if ABC is related to Able. ABC is not an institutional lender and is really rendering no financial services to the partnership. The \$7,000 consulting fee is also a syndication fee if Consultants, Inc. is related to Able or any entity that is related to Able.

4. The selling commissions of \$28,000, payable to licensed real estate brokers and salesmen also represents a syndication fee, even though Able may not directly profit by it. The \$28,000, after all, is not applied toward reducing the purchase price of the property. Further, many syndicators are willing to absorb such selling commissions themselves.

5. Thus, the \$75,000 of proceeds that is not applied toward

a reduction in the purchase price of the property or operation of the property represents syndication fees if Able is related in any way to the other groups involved in the syndication process. Further, the $100,000 pure markup is a hidden syndication fee if such a relationship exists. It is even possible that part of the syndicates $400,000 down payment might involve a hidden real estate commission. Therefore, the investor should inquire from Able whether there are any real estate commissions involved in either of the purchase transactions described in the offering circular, and, if so, whether Able or any related group is going to receive the commission or commissons.

CONCLUSION

Several general observations can be made concerning the fairness of syndication fees. First, the dollar amounts of the fees should be reasonable in light of the syndicator's time, effort, financial risks, and the size and nature of the investment. Second, the fees should be structured to provide ample incentives for the syndicator to be conscientious in the acquisition, management, and resale of the investment. Finally, the fee structure should assure compatibility and mutuality of interests between the syndicator and the investor. If the syndicator profits, his investors should also profit. To the extent the above elements are present within the fee structure, the greater the safety, security, and profit potential that will accompany your investment.

5

How to Determine the Real Value of the Investment Property

Like many people seeking to take advantage of the potentially great rewards of real estate investment, you probably know something about the market. It's hard to be totally ignorant. Dinner conversations, newspaper articles, magazine columns, and even television specials are continually discussing, debating, and rehashing current events in the real estate world.

But the information that can make you casually conversant with real estate is not sufficient to support you when the time comes to risk your money in a syndicated investment. There is a vast difference between knowing that prices are rising and knowing whether or not the high price of the property a syndicator is touting is justified. This is particularly true in a hot market. Because there are many syndicators around but, comparatively speaking, few properties suitable for syndicate investment, those pieces of real estate that draw the attention of syndicators can become the center of competitive bidding that forces prices up beyond reason. Thus, a syndicator who is trying to encourage you to invest may be holding property whose price is not based on a sound, rational economic base.

It is essential, therefore, that you be able to determine, independently and without pressure, the value of a piece of property offered by a syndicator for your consideration.

Although there are any number of methods that can be used to evaluate property, I have outlined the most commonly used —the gross multiplier, net income, cost of replacement, comparable sales, and independent appraisals. Each has its merits and faults. But if you subject the property offered you to several of the methods and then compare the value assessment each yields, you should get a reasonably good idea of what the property is worth.

GROSS MULTIPLIER METHOD OF VALUATION

One of the more rudimentary approaches to the evaluation of property is that its worth is equal to the yearly rental income, multiplied by a "magic" number or gross multiplier. For example, if an apartment building is being sold for $700,000 and if the current owner can show yearly gross receipts of $100,000, the value of the building can be said to fall within a "seven times gross" multiplier.

I wish I could name a specific number, say seven, and tell you that it is *the* infallible gross multiplier. But in truth, there is not one single multiplier applicable to all situations. The gross multiplier you use to determine what a property may be worth will depend on several factors:

1. The quality and type of construction.
2. The area of the country where you live. The area where the property is located within your city.
3. Who the tenants are.
4. The age of the property.
5. Whether the property is furnished or unfurnished.
6. Whether the landlord or the tenants pay for utilities.

Although it may seem to you that you might as well pick a number out of a hat and use that as a multiplier, let me assure you that there is a degree of rationality in the method. As you grow more sophisticated as a real estate investor, you will find that you will be able to determine with fair accuracy what multiplier you use for what property. (Almost immediately, for example, you'll come to understand that a newer building, an unfurnished building, or an adults-only building will have a higher gross multiplier than a building that takes children or a building with furnished apartments.) But until that day comes, you can find out what multiplier to use by interviewing several real estate professionals in your area.

The gross multiplier method is based on the premise that certain properties entail relatively constant operating expenses and that the important factor to be considered by the investor is the gross income. Although I feel this premise is quite suspect, it has nevertheless gained wide acceptance, and because many people (including the investors who may come along later to buy the property from your syndicate) rely on the gross multiplier method, using it yourself will help you make sure that the purchase price falls within a price range considered reasonable (or unreasonable, for that matter) by others.

But, assuming that you want to be smarter than other investors around you, be advised that the gross multiplier method is risky. It often can lead you to a valuation that exceeds the true value of the property, primarily because the gross receipts offered up for evaluation may not be all they seem to be. This is particularly true of buildings that are still in the construction stage. If the syndicate you are interested in joining is one that is eyeing an apartment or office complex that is barely off the ground, you should be cautious when the builder or syndicator quotes the expected gross receipts once the building is finished and rented. Of necessity, the gross receipt estimate is only that, an estimate, and a highly chancy one at that.

Similarly, you must be careful if you are about to get involved with a building that has just been opened for rentals but is not fully occupied. Here also the quotations of gross receipts may be overstated. Consider the following situations:

First, that an aggressive builder will, for example, price *all* units in a new complex within a narrow, but high, price range. That is, in an apartment building, the two-bedroom units might be priced $390, $395, and $400. The prime units, those with a view, those away from street noise, those without neighbors, will rent first and for the highest prices. The builder will try to tell you that receipts from these first rentals are indicative of what can be expected when the building is full. This is not so. The gross receipt estimates based on early rentals will be deceptive because in time the builder will have to cut prices if the remaining units are to be rented. The two-bedroom apartments overlooking the alley, those next to the common laundry rooms, or those across from the elevators will surely go for lower rents. Using a gross multiplier on the builder's early receipts, in other words, would yield an inflated value for the building.

Second, even if the books show that the apartments or office spaces have been leased, say, for an average of $400 a month for one year, you have no guarantee that the money flowing in actually represents gross receipts. In order to lure tenants to the building, the builder may have had to make considerable concessions. For example, the tenants may have been promised that they could live in their apartments for two months without paying rent and that their leases would actually begin at the end of the two free months. Therefore, each tenant would have a 14-month occupancy and each lease, reflecting only 12 months of rent receipts, would be overstated by more than 16 percent. Again, applying the multiplier to the seller's figures would yield an inflated value for the building.

NET INCOME APPROACH TO EVALUATING PROPERTY

Personally, I don't think you should base a decision to invest money in a syndicate solely on the results of a gross multiplier evaluation.

The gross multiplier gives you a rough idea of what the property is worth. But, if you are to be a sophisticated investor, you also may want to look into real estate syndicates for the most basic and soundest of economic reasons: To obtain a good annual cash return on your money. Because return on invested capital should be your most important goal, you should try to evaluate a piece of syndicated property according to the net income it is likely to generate. For this kind of an evaluation, the gross multiplier is worthless because it does not take into consideration how mortgage costs, utility expenses, vacancy rates, and property taxes are going to bite into the anticipated receipts. The gross multiplier, in other words, does not tell you precisely how much of a cash flow you can anticipate when buying into a piece of real estate.

Before you launch on a net value assessment, you have to decide, of course, what kind of a return you want on the money you are going to put into the syndicate. Once you have decided that (let's say you want to make 8 percent on the money you have set aside for the syndicate) you can use the following formula to compute what price the syndicate (and by extension, you) should be paying for the property if it is to help you reach your investment goal.

GI = Gross income at full occupancy
E = Operating expenses (including vacancy and maintenance allowances)
L = Total of all loans against the property
DS = Annual debt service
CF = Annual cash flow
CI = Cash investment
R = Expected cash return as percentage of cash investment
P = Price or market value

From the above, we can compute several important formulas, which are as follows:

$$GI - E - DS = CF$$
$$CF \div R = CI$$
$$CI + L = P$$

Let's see how this formula works under a given set of facts. Assume the following:

$GI = \$75{,}000$
$E = \$30{,}000$
$L = \$400{,}000$
$DS = \$35{,}000$
$R = 8\%$

At what price should the syndicate be buying the property? How much of a down payment should the syndicator make if you and the other investors are to earn an 8 percent return on invested cash?

Let's take	Gross income	$ 75,000
And subtract	Operating expenses	30,000
And	Annual debt service	35,000
Which leaves you an	Annual cash flow	$ 10,000
Now, let's take the	Cash flow	10,000
And divide by	Expected cash return as percentage of cash investment	0.08
Which yields a	Cash investment	$125,000
Which added to the	Existing loans against property	400,000
Tells you the amount of the	Purchase price	$525,000

Generally speaking, if the syndicator pays more than \$525,000 and makes more than a \$125,000 down payment, the syndicate will not make an 8 percent return on its investment. And neither will you.[1]

Something that has always bothered me about the net income method is that it can distort the value of the property, especially if it is being financed at a time of exceptionally high-interest rates. For example, you might be considering a property and decide that it would be a bad investment even if it is well located and nicely constructed. Why? Because in your computation of net income, you might be taking into consideration a current 10 percent loan under which the syndicate is buying the property. But keep in mind that the effect of a bad loan can be mitigated or even eliminated entirely by refinancing the property at a later time, when interest rates have fallen. Thus, if you are investing during a tight money market, you may want to work your way through the net value formula by using a debt service figure that takes into consideration the more moderate interest rates that are likely to prevail when money becomes more easily available later. In fact, some real estate professionals valuate property without taking debt service into consideration at all. Under the no-debt service concept, cash flow before debts service in the example above would be *GI* (\$75,000) less *E* (\$30,000), or \$45,000. \$45,000 divided by 0.08 would yield you a net value of \$562,500.

Any formula, of course, is only as good as the reliability of the component figures it includes. If you want it to work for you, you have to be sure that you are not overstating, understating, or misstating any of the variables particular to your investment. Look back at the example we just worked and assume that our "investor" overlooked a recent increase in property taxes and utilities costs that had raised operating expenses to \$35,000 (not the \$30,000 cited). Under those circumstances, the cash flow would really be \$5,000 (not \$10,000), the cash investment would fall to \$62,500 (\$5,000/0.08) and the value would be \$462,500. Our investor, in other words, would have

---

[1] These are broad stroke figures. While you may set a certain percentage goal for yourself when you invest, your actual return will be somewhat smaller because, as the following chapters indicate, other costs will bear on your investment.

miscalculated the true worth of the property by $62,500—and would have had a rude shock when returns on the investment failed to live up to expectations.

APPRAISALS

Trying to determine how much a piece of real estate is really worth is no easy job—especially for a beginner. Thus, even if you have made your own gross multiplier evaluation and have worked your way through to a net income evaluation, you might feel better, and on safer ground, if you get some independent confirmation of the conclusions you have reached. One way to do this is to obtain an independent appraisal of the property offered by the syndicator.

Some syndicators may give you an appraisal. Some, because they have organized public syndications and are required to issue independent appraisals before regulatory agencies will issue permits to sell syndicate interests. Independent appraisals supplied by the syndicator can be helpful. But never forget that no matter how thorough those appraisals may seem, they are likely to contain bias toward the syndicator because it is the syndicator who has selected and paid the appraiser.

I don't think that you should accept any syndicator's appraisal of a property without question.

If the syndicator is obtaining a new loan to purchase the property, the lender will have made its own appraisal of the project's worth. Ask the syndicator for a copy of the lender's appraisal. If the syndicator tells you the appraisal was informal and that nothing was committed to writing, approach the lender directly. Since, traditionally, lenders cast a conservative eye on property they are about to finance, the lender's valuation will be especially important and useful to you.

Should the lender refuse to cooperate (which lenders sometimes do), you still have options. Each savings and loan institution has guidelines that determine how much it will loan for different types of property. For example, while a lender may loan as much as 80 percent (in California) toward the purchase of a new home, it may advance only 75 percent toward the purchase of an apartment building. You know the amount the lender has committed (or is willing to commit) to the property. If you can then learn the percentage of total value the lender makes available, you can compute what the lender's appraised value of the property is. For eaxmple, if you know the property was financed for $400,000 by a lender that advances 75 percent of appraised value, you know that you are looking at a piece of real estate valued at $533,333.

However, in following this method, you must tread lightly. For example, the syndicator, rather than negotiating for a new loan, may simply be picking up the existing loan on the property. If you use the existing loan as a base for your calculations, the value you arrive at will, in all probability, be too low because over the intervening years, property values will have climbed. Thus, you should complement a valuation based on the lender's commitment with an assessment of how much other similar properties in the same area have risen (or fallen, for that matter) in the years since the loan on your property was made.

Also, be absolutely sure that your information about the amount and percentage of the loan is precise. Don't ask a loan officer at the savings and loan, "How much do you loan on apartment buildings?" and let it go at that. The officer may tell you, "We usually loan 75 percent." But, it may well be that the current owner, for assorted reasons, received only a 60 percent loan. When you ask, therefore, be sure you specify what property you have in mind.

If you are successful in your quest, you are in a superior position to make a decision. If the appraised value, as seen by the lender and adjusted for reasonable variables, comes close to the figure you have established independently, you are in business. If you find that there is a wide gap between the appraised value and the price for which the property has been offered to the syndicate, you know that you had better be careful and look further into the possible reasons for the wide divergence.

Finally, if you just can't get an independent appraisal from the syndicator or lender, you may have one source left. You can go to the tax assessor's office and look up the value the property has been given for tax purposes. This is information that is public and readily available to you. However, the tax assessor's valuation of property is usually less than market value and is often out of date. So the information, while open to you, may not be altogether helpful.

EVALUATING PROPERTY ACCORDING TO COMPARABLE SALES

If you have the time and the inclination to do some extensive "leg" work, you can try to assess the value of a syndicator's offering by looking around the area where the syndicator's property is located and determining the recent selling price of comparable projects. You can do this by consulting with real estate brokers in the area. Also, you can do it by checking sale records filed with the appropriate agency (like the county clerk) in your area.

A syndicator may try to tell you that it is impossible to make comparisons. But, if you are willing to make the effort, you can indeed come up with comparable sale figures. Your biggest problem, in fact, will be to take into consideration the variables that must inevitably creep into your computations. The property offered by your syndicator may have subterranean parking. Other buildings recently sold in the area may not have had the convenience. You'll have to decide how much weight to give to the difference. On the other hand, other buildings may have had game rooms, an amenity missing from your syndicator's building. Again, how much difference that should make in the values is something you will have to decide.

EVALUATION ACCORDING TO COST OF REPLACEMENT

Some sellers, realtors and syndicators may try to tell you that you can estimate the value of a property by determining how much it would cost to replace. Superficially, it is an attractive argument. But, given the high rate of inflation, especially over the last few years, it is obvious that replacing almost any building will exceed its purchase price, but that doesn't make it more valuable. Cost replacement does not consider the revenues and expenses the property involves and, therefore, it is of little value in helping you estimate net cash return on invested capital. It does not allow you to take into consideration where the property is located and it does not allow you to assess realistically the value of the land itself. It is, in short, not a good way to cast a critical eye on a property.

A CASE STUDY

The methods of evaluation I have discussed above can be best understood if applied to an actual situation. Let's look at an investment syndicated a few years ago in the west Los Angeles area and, assuming that you are interested in participating as an investor, let's see how the property can be analyzed with the help of the various approaches to value assessment.

Your starting point is the information presented in the following prospectus which the syndicator has prepared for interested investors:

BARTON PROPERTIES, LTD., INVESTMENT

Barton Properties, Ltd., a California limited partnership (the "Partnership") is being formed to acquire a newly constructed 22-unit unfurnished apartment building located in west Los Angeles. The three-story apartment building has a full security system, including a closed-circuit television system and intercom from each apartment unit to the apartment entrance. The building features a large recreation room with complete kitchen facilities. The individual apartment units feature built-in dishwashers, ovens, intercoms, large closets, air conditioning and radiant heating. Some units have gas fireplaces.

The building consists of approximately 16,000 square feet of rentable space, and 4,000 square feet of common areas. The land upon which the building is situated consists of approximately 18,000 square feet, and is valued at $8 per square foot.

The purchase price of the property is $640,000, with a $175,000 cash down payment. The balance of the purchase price is represented by a 30-year first trust deed (mortgage) of $465,000 bearing interest at 8.5 percent per annum, payable $3,575 per month. Projected gross annual rents from the building are $86,000, with operating expenses estimated to be $32,000 per year, and the vacancy factor estimated to be 5 percent.

Gross Multiplier Valuation

In order to compute the gross multiplier for the above investment you divide the purchase price of $640,000 by the projected gross annual rents of $86,000, and arrive at a gross multiplier of 7.44. In order to verify the computed gross multiplier, you should check other comparable apartment buildings in the same area and determine whether rents from similar units are more or less equal to those projected in the syndicator's brochure for the offered property. Assuming that the computed gross multiplier proves to be accurate, you then must determine whether the gross multiplier for your building falls within the range of gross multipliers for similar buildings in the area. Again, this requires independent investigation or consultations with knowledgeable real estate professionals. Don't forget that there may be factors that can account for a higher gross multiplier on your prospective investment: the building may be newer, may be in better shape, have a more desirable location, have more amenities, and may be for adults only.

Net Income Valuation

To appraise the investment according to net income, you have to project the net cash flow for the building. From gross income of $86,000, you must first subtract the estimated $32,000 operating expenses. Then, because the building is only 95 percent filled during the year, you must subtract the amount of rent lost as a result of the 5 percent vacancy. In this case, lost rentals amount to $4,300. Finally, you must deduct the annual mortgage loan payments (the monthly mortgage of $3,575 multiplied by 12), which is $42,900. After all these deductions, the annual net cash flow comes to $6,800.

Now you must determine what kind of a cash return on your investment is reasonable under current market conditions. If prevailing apartment investments are likely to pay you about 5 percent on invested capital, you should expect that the syndicated investment should return a similar amount. Therefore, you compute the property's value as follows:

Net cash flow	$ 6,800
Expected cash return	÷ 0.05
Cash investment	$136,000
Amount of loan	465,000
Estimated value	$601,000

The syndicate's purchase price of $640,000, in other words, seems to be somewhat high (assuming, of course, that projected rents and expenses are accurate).

You must, of course, realize that most new apartment projects (like the one offered in this investment opportunity) generate very little, if any, positive cash flow during the first few years of operation. Therefore, if you want to evaluate your investment according to net income, you might want to adjust the formula so that it substitutes an *anticipated* cash flow figure for the current cash flow. You may, for example, decide that the offered building will yield a net annual cash flow of $15,000 after two years of operation. The net valuation will then come to $765,000 ($15,000 cash flow divided by 0.05 which yields a cash investment of $300,000. That, plus the loan amount of $465,000 equals $765,000). Of course, a major risk in anticipating conditions two years hence is that there can be changes in market conditions that would work against you. At that time, for example, buyers may be looking for a 7 percent return on capital. If your syndicate tries to resell its property, the value of your building, according to the net income formula, would be $679,285, and not the $765,000 you might have projected.

Replacement Cost Valuation

To evaluate the Barton property according to replacement cost, you must first determine present costs of construction for similar buildings. Architects and building contractors would be your best source of information.

They might tell you, for example, that the cost of constructing a building like the one you are considering as an investment is $25 per square foot for the space to be rented and $18 per square foot for the so-called common areas like the lobby or recreation room. Your computations would then run as follows:

16,000 feet of rentable space at $25 a square foot.	$400,000
4,000 feet of common areas at $18 a square foot.	72,000
Cost of building.	$472,000
Cost of land (which you have found is about $8 a square foot in the west Los Angeles area).	144,000
Total cost.	$616,000

The difference between the replacement value and the price at which the syndicator is offering the property may mean that the property is overvalued. But it may also mean that the difference is attributable to the costs of the syndication process (see Chapter 6).

As I mentioned before, this method of evaluating property has its limitations because it takes into account neither revenues nor expenses.

Lender's Appraised Value

According to the prospectus offered by the syndicator, a savings and loan institution will lend $465,000 on a first trust deed against the property. By contacting the loan officer directly, you may find out what percentage of the appraised value the lender commits to properties like the one being syndicated. If the lender's policy, at the time the loan commitment was made, was to fund 75 percent of appraised value, simple calculation will tell you that the lender believes the property to be worth $620,000.

Remember, however, that lending institutions make conservative appraisals. Thus, the $20,000 difference between the syndicator's figure and the lender's estimate should not make you uneasy. The red flag should go up in your mind only when there is a substantial difference between the lender's appraised value and the selling price of the proprty.

Because there are so many variables in appraising property, I cannot emphasize strongly enough that you consult as much as possible with experienced and informed real estate professionals about the property you are being offered through a syndicate. Professionals are often willing to share useful data about sales trends, rental market conditions, and location factors.

No matter what price your various calculations yield, you must also take into consideration the syndicator behind the offering. An experienced, competent syndicator can take a mismanaged and poorly maintained property and turn it into a solid and advantageous investment by reducing expenses and increasing rents. An unskilled syndicator can take the best value in town and turn it into a financial disaster.

6

How to Determine the Real Cost of Your Investment

Although determining the fair market value of an investment property is an essential step toward deciding whether or not to participate in a specific syndicate, even the most accurate value assessment you can possibly undertake will not provide you with the base you need to make a final, intelligent decision.

At any given time, there are scores of real estate syndicators who are willing, indeed eager, to include you in their plans. But, you will not be able to judge whether the yield—your net cash flow as a percentage of invested capital—from one syndicate is likely to be better or worse than your yield from another investment syndicate until you learn to evaluate the real cost of any opportunity offered to you.

By real cost I mean the purchase price for the property *plus* the syndication and property acquisition costs: These may include:

1. The fees the syndicators charge for their services.
2. Real estate commissions, if not already included in the purchase price.
3. The cost of raising the money the syndicator needs to make the investment a reality. This includes commissions to sales agents who find investors, the costs of printing offering brochures and circulars, and costs related to promoting the syndicate.
4. Expenses for organizing the syndicate, particularly legal and accounting fees.

5. Those expenses that arise with public offerings such as filing and appraisal fees, and legal and accounting costs.
6. Expenses that arise as the property is acquired such as escrow costs, loan costs and fees, title insurance premiums and, again, legal and accounting fees.
7. Any expenditures that might be necessary to bring the property up to the break-even point. This may mean paying for repairs, refurbishing, and newspaper rental advertisements. It may also mean contributing money to a fund to cover expected operational deficits.
8. In some cases, the real cost of your investment may be increased by the purported tax benefits of the investment. For example, many syndicators tout prepaid interest and loan fees as "extra" benefits that "flow through" to the investor to use as tax write-offs. But since actual payments must be made, the benefits are not quite as "free" as some syndicators would like to make them seem, and must be counted as additions to the real cost of the investment.

SOME CASE STUDIES

This chapter, hopefully, will do several things. It will teach you how to identify any or all of the expenditures mentioned above and to use them to calculate the real cost of any syndicate investment you have in mind. It will show you how these costs dilute the current yield of your investment. It will help you determine whether or not the syndication costs and their effects on your potential investment are justified in light of current market yields for other similar properties. It will also show you how an understanding of real costs can help you assess the investment's downside risk and calculate the potential return if the property appreciates in value.

The best way to learn to compute the real cost of your investment is to look at some actual syndicated investments (reproduced below in modified form) and see how real cost calculations are made.

Investment 1

> Casa Bonita Associates, Ltd. a limited partnership, (the Partnership) is being formed to acquire a new 35-unit apart-

ment building located in San Diego, California. The purchase price is $1 million, with a $300,000 cash down payment, and a new $700,000 first trust deed loan. The bank will charge an additional $7,000 fee for the loan.

Able Management, the general partner of the Partnership, will receive a $50,000 syndication fee for organizing the syndicate and for supervising the rent-up phase of the apartment building. In addition, $20,000 in commissions will be paid to the licensed real estate salesmen who will sell the limited partnership interests. Five thousand dollars will be spent to cover legal, accounting, and other organizational expenses of the Partnership. . . .

Projected net cash flow from the property is $21,000, after payment of all operational expenses and debt service. . . .

What is the real cost of the above investment? Start with the stated purchase price of $1 million. Then add the costs of the syndication and acquisition processes, which are as follows:

Syndication fee	$50,000
Salesmen's commissions	20,000
Organizational costs	5,000
Loan fee	7,000
Total	$82,000

Thus, the real cost of the investment is $1 million plus $82,000, or $1,082,000.

Investment 2

De Anza Plaza Investors, Ltd. (the Partnership) is being formed to acquire a 30,000 squart foot shopping center located in Houston, Texas. The purchase price of the shopping center is $700,000, with a cash down payment of $125,000, and the balance of the purchase price represented by a first trust deed in favor of the seller. The shopping center is ten years old, and in need of renovation. Present gross income is $80,000, and present net cash flow is $7,000. . . .

Build-Right Construction Company, the general partner of the Partnership, will supervise the refurbishing of the shopping center at a projected cost of $125,000. Renovation will include general repair work on the exterior portions of the center, repaving the parking area, and converting the design

> of the center to a Spanish motif. Thereafter, the general partner will be responsible for re-leasing the center's shops at an anticipated 30 percent increase in rents. For its services, the general partner will receive a contractor's fee of $25,000, and a first year's management fee of $10,000. In addition, the general partner will be entitled to a 15 percent equity participation share in the Partnership for its time and effort in organizing the Partnership and acquiring the shopping center. . . .
>
> It is expected that there will be $30,000 in operating deficits during the refurbishing and rent-up phases of the investment. . . .

What is the real cost of the above investment? Again, we start with the $700,000 purchase price. To that, we add the following costs:

Refurbishing cost	$125,000
Contractor's fee	25,000
Management fee	10,000
Operating deficits	30,000
Total	$190,000

However, in this case, adding the various costs of renovating and managing the property ($190,000) to the price of the shopping center ($700,000) does not yet yield the real cost of the investment. Remember that the prospectus tells us that the syndicator will take a 15 percent share in the investment as an additional fee for organizing the syndicate partnership and acquiring the shopping center. You and your fellow investors will have to bear the cost of the syndicator's equity. The calculation is based on invested capital. In the above case, that means invested capital of $315,000 ($125,000 down payment + $190,000 renovations costs) = 85 percent of the total equity. Total equity = $315,000/.85, or $370,588, and the syndicator's equity = 15 percent × $370,588, or $55,588. That $55,588 becomes part of the cost. Therefore, the real cost of the investment is $700,000 + $190,000 + $55,588 = $945,588.

Real Cost and Investment Yield

Property 1. Once you have computed the real cost of the syndicate investment you are drawn to, you are in a position to determine how this real cost will affect the current yield of the property.

Let's take another look at the first investment we studied above.

At first blush the current yield on the property seems to be 7 percent: the $300,000 down payment required to obtain the property would yield a $21,000 net cash flow.

But, since the investors in the syndicate will have to contribute an additional $82,000 to cover syndication and acquisition costs, the total cash paid out for the property comes to $382,000. If we refigure the yield, we see that the $21,000 net cash flow represents only a 5.5 ($21,000/$382,000) percent return on cash invested.

Property 2. Evaluating the effect of real cost on the yield of investment 2 is somewhat more difficult. The high real costs would seem to presage a low annual cash return on investment. On the other hand, the very purpose of the high costs is to increase the current yield by making the property more attractive, thereby increasing the rentals it can command—in this case 30 percent, from $80,000 to $104,000 a year.

If we assume that operating expenses will remain relatively constant (which should be the case), we can make the following calculations:

Net cash flow	= $ 7,000 (present cash flow)
	= $ 24,000 (increased revenues)
Expected cash flow	= $ 31,000
Invested capital	= $125,000 down payment + 190,000 refurbishing costs
	= $315,000
True yield	= $ 31,000/$315,000 × 0.85* = 0.836

* Remember, the syndicator has the other 15 percent.

In other words, while the immediate yield is 5.6 percent (a return of $7,000 on the $125,000 down payment on an "as is" property) the expected yield could rise to 8.36 percent, even when refurbishing costs are included.

Is the Yield Reasonable?

Whatever the nature of your syndicated investment, whether it resembles the property outlined in the first or second example, you must ask yourself whether the true yield of your potential investment is reasonable.

By talking with real estate appraisers, brokers, and other professionals, as well as with experienced investors, you should determine how much comparable investments elsewhere are yielding. If you find that the yield of your investment is comparable to other investment yields, you can feel comfortable with the syndicate you have in mind.

But what if your projected yield is lower than those available elsewhere? Does that mean you should abandon the idea of investing in the syndicate?

Not necessarily. Although you must make the final decision, I think there are times when you can settle for a yield that is up to 1 or even 2 percent lower than other yields, especially if you find that there are advantages other than the immediate dollar and cents return. It may be that your syndicator is particularly knowledgeable and may be able to negotiate better terms of purchase for the property. Perhaps indications are that the syndicator is likely to manage the property in superior fashion. Perhaps the property offered is in a highly desirable area and is of a high quality. All of these factors, you could calculate, may mean that in the long run, your syndicate's property may appreciate significantly in value. Under these circumstances you may be perfectly justified in settling for a smaller monetary yield. You should abandon an investment only when its yield is significantly less than the yield you might gain by placing your money elsewhere.

If the yield on an investment like the one we discussed in Example 1 is very much higher than yields available elsewhere, you have one strong positive factor to include in your decision-making process. But what if property 2's yield is higher than similar projects? Is that yield a strong positive factor as well?

That depends on you. In this case, other factors may come into play. An investment in a to-be-refurbished property is one that entails higher risk. You must decide whether the high yield you have been promised is sufficiently high to induce you to take a chance that the syndicator will indeed be able to increase rents by 30 percent. You may find that it is not. Or, other investments may be returning less, but may not entail as great a risk. But you must also remember that in a time of rising property values, the poorly managed and maintained property offers a syndicate its best opportunity for buying real estate without having to pay top dollar. This in turn means that the property, if properly renovated and managed, has a greater potential for appreciation than real estate your syndicate might have bought in first-class shape.

Real Cost and Downside Risk

Knowing the real cost of your investment will enable you to calculate the investment's downside risk. In some cases, the figuring will not have to be especially complicated. If we look at the property we studied in the first example, we see that its purchase price is $1 million. Since the additional costs are relatively modest in this case—only $82,000—you can anticipate that even in a moderately increasing market it will not take long to reach the break-even point.

In other cases, however, the syndication and acquisition processes will give the investment a real cost that far exceeds the fair market value of the property. In the second example we analyzed, for example, the real cost of the property is a substantial $237,250 greater than its market value at the time of purchase. It is obvious that in this case there is a potential for greater loss if the property does not live up to promise or, if worse, the syndicator's plans go awry and the property must be resold under adverse conditions.

In either case, you should also calculate how much the property must appreciate if it is to reach the break-even point. In the case of the first investment, the market would only have to rise 8.2 percent ($82,000/$1,000,000) in order to ensure that the syndicate's (and your) investment will not lose money. In the second case it must rise .35 percent ($245,588/$700,000) to guarantee the investors a cushion against loss.

Real Cost and Appreciation in Value

Calculating the real cost of your investment will also provide you with a yardstick with which you can measure the real expected return on your investment.

Let's assume that you are investing in a property like the one in the first example. Let's also assume that all your inquiries and research have shown that your investment should appreciate at the rate of 10 percent a year and that the syndicator has told you that the property will be sold at the end of four years. Your expected return may be calculated as follows:

Original purchase price	$1,000,000
Appreciation factor (40%)	400,000
Selling price	$1,400,000
Less estimated selling commissions (5%)	70,000
Net proceeds from sale	$1,330,000
Less real cost	($1,082,000)
Total Appreciation	$ 248,000

Percent Return on invested dollars = 64.92%
248,000/382,000*
Average annual return = 16.23%†

* $300,000 down payment plus $82,000 syndication and acquisition costs.

† The above return does not take into account the income tax consequences of the sale. However, it also does not include the return on investment due to income tax benefits, cash flow distributions, and equity buildup.

The figures above show a fair return on investment. However, as you judge this example and your own future syndicate investment possibilities, remember that you should look upon appreciation in value (and therefore potential return on your money) in light of the *total* invested capital (down payment of $300,000 plus $82,000 in cost of syndication process) and not only in relation to cash down payment. This is important because profits as a percentage of total invested capital will be smaller than profits as a percentage of cash down payment. When you assess the potential return of your investment, it is this return-as-a-percentage-of-total-invested capital that must determine whether you put your money into this syndicate, another syndicate, a savings certificate, the stock market, government bonds, or some other investment.

DISGUISING THE REAL COST—A SYNDICATOR'S PLOY

Because the effort to determine the real cost of a syndicated offering can go a long way toward making you a more sophisticated investor, some syndicators may try to short-circuit your calculations by telling you that you should really be giving greater consideration to something they call "net investment cost."

The syndicator who tries this approach is basing his selling pitch on the theory that your capital contribution to the syndication is reduced by the tax benefits that you can expect to reap in the first year of your investment. For example, let's assume that you are in the 50 percent tax bracket, that you are prepared to invest $10,000 in a syndication, and that, according to the figures presented, your investment will qualify you for a $6,000 tax write-off. The syndicator may tell you that the whole transaction should be viewed as if you had only invested $7,000. That is:

Your investment	$10,000
50 percent of $6,000 in write-offs	3,000
"Net" investment	$ 7,000

Since it appears that there has been a 30 percent reduction in the cost of your investment, the syndicator will also tell you, the property will only have to resold at a price that nets you $7,000 in order for you to break even.

However, I think that the net investment cost argument is misleading. First, when you join a syndicate, you do so in order to obtain all the benefits the syndicate has to offer. This means that, among other things, you should get a full tax savings benefit and a full appreciation benefit. Pooling the two benefits (as you would do in this case) means that you get the full value of neither.

Second, net investment cost calculations make it hard, if not impossible, to compare the benefits offered by the syndicate that uses this approach with the benefits offered by a syndicate that calculates costs in a more conventional fashion. If you are going to make a wise investment decision, you must be in a position to compare each and every benefit on a one to one basis.

Third, net investment cost approach distorts the profitability of the syndicate. If you contribute $10,000 to a syndicate that projects a $20,000 return, you assume that you will have made a 100 percent profit. But if you give $10,000 to a syndicator who says that you are really investing only $7,000 and that you stand to reap a $20,000 return, you will mistakenly think that you will be making a 185 percent return on the invested capital.

Thus, if a syndicator presents you with a fact and figure sheet that features the net cost investment method, my advice is to rework the material presented and judge promised tax benefits, annual cash returns, and profit on sale according to your actual invested dollars.

To summarize: Determining and applying the "real cost" of your prospective syndicate investments will prove to be an extremely valuable tool. With it, you will be able to assess the downside risk of various investments, to measure the apprecia- tion in the investments, and to analyze the way in which the yields from these investments compare.

7

Financing: The Key to Profits

Gross income. Cash flow. The syndicator. Tax write-offs. Syndication fees. Location of property. The list of variables that can affect the viability of a syndicated real estate investment is long and complex. While you may be tempted to give all the factors equal weight in deliberating a particular offering, one variable should merit special attention; that is, the type and nature of the financial arrangements the syndicator has made (or is making) to buy the property.

Financing affects the point at which the syndicate breaks even on its investment. Financing bears strongly on the amount of cash that can be distributed to the investors every year. It controls the rate at which equity in the property builds up during the time the syndicate holds the property. Financing influences the profit you will make when the syndicate resells the property.

In short, if the syndicator has financed the property soundly, it is likely that your investment will be profitable and safe.

THE COMPONENTS OF REAL ESTATE FINANCING

Interest Rates

If you are to make an incisive analysis of the potential in a specific real estate investment, you must compare its financing arrangements with those of other available syndicate investments. One important variable is the interest rate. The lower the interest rate, the smaller the mortgage payments and, therefore, the higher the net cash flow. Moreover, if the syndicator has managed to obtain the lowest possible interest rate under the existing money market conditions, the property will, in all likelihood, command a higher price—and return higher profits —when it is resold.

Several years ago, two syndicates with which I was familiar each bought an apartment house. The two buildings were almost identical in size, amenities offered, and location. Each syndicate paid approximately $750,000 for its building. The down payment in each case was $150,000 cash. Syndicate A was able to assume an existing 30-year, $600,000 loan at 8 percent interest. Syndicate B, however, had to obtain a new loan at 9 percent.

As a result, Syndicate A paid $52,920 a year to cover its loan obligation while Syndicate B had to pay $57,360. For Syndicate A, lower payments brought multiple rewards. Because loan payments were smaller (comparatively speaking) the break-even point for operating the building was lower. The 1 percent difference in the interest rates resulted in an additional $4,440 to distribute to the investors. Syndicate A's investors, in other words, received 3 percent more on their invested capital ($4,440/$150,000) than Syndicate B's investors.

Because both loans were assignable, each syndicate, upon selling its property, could pass its loan along to the new buyer. Although this was a plus for both syndicates, Syndicate A, because it had a lower interest rate, benefited even more. When both properties went on the market, Syndicate A was able to command $44,000 more in price and in the cash down payment. Why? Because investors at that time were looking for a 10 percent return on their capital. Since Syndicate A's building was capable of generating $4,400 more in cash flow, an additional payment of $44,000 was economically justified.

Amortization Period

A syndicate's (and therefore your) profits from an investment will also be influenced by the length of time over which the loan on the property is amortized. Generally speaking, the longer the amortization period, the greater the amount of money is available after operating expenses for distribution to the investors.

In the example discussed above, Syndicate A had an edge over B because the former had a loan with a lower interest rate. But let's assume for a moment that A's 8 percent loan had been issued for 20 years while B's 9 percent loan had borne an amortization period of 30 years. Under these circumstances, Syndicate A would have had to pay $60,228 a year for its loan. But Syndicate B would have had to pay only $57,936 a year. In other words, B's property would have returned a higher cash flow to investors than A.

Keep in mind one additional fact. A good syndicator will sometimes use amortization periods to increase cash flow by refinancing an existing loan and increasing the time over which the debt on the property is amortized. One syndicator I know bought a building that had an existing 12-year amortization loan. He immediately refinanced the property with a larger loan, spread over 25 years. Because the new loan was larger, he was able to give the investors back 30 percent of the capital they had invested to purchase the property. Even though the new loan was larger, the longer amortization period reduced the amount of the yearly payments. As a result, the syndicator was also able to generate an additional 5 percent on invested capital.

When you weigh the effects of amortization be sure, however, that you know the precise difference between the amortization period and the term of the loan. The amortization period determines the amount of yearly loan payments. The loan term determines the date by which the entire loan must be fully paid. If the amortization period and the loan term are the same, well and good. However, many loans today are made for periods of time that are *shorter* than the amortization period. That means that at the end of the loan term, a balloon payment will have to be made to make up the difference between the amount already amortized and the original loan amount.

Equity Buildup Considerations

The interest your syndicate is paying on its loan can have considerable impact on your equity in the property. The lower the interest rate, the larger the portion of the annual payments allocated to diminishing the loan principal. Thus, when the syndicate sells the property, a larger share of the proceeds of the sale is available for distribution to the investors because less money must be earmarked to pay off the remaining debt to the lender.

You should keep in mind, however, that equity buildup, while important, does take second place to the impact the interest rate and the amortization period have on the day-to-day costs of operating the property. Look on equity buildup as a bonus rather than a prime benefit of favorable financing.

Transferability Provisions

Some lenders will make loans that do not have due-on-sale clauses (also known as alienation clauses). In essence that means that the loan can be passed on to a new buyer when the property is sold without additional loan fees or increase in interest rates. This can be of tremendous advantage if the syndicate obtains a loan during times of easy money (when interest rates are likely to be low) and sells the property when the money market is tighter, and interest rates are up. If your syndicate can hold out the promise that a low-interest loan can be freely assumed, it can ask a higher price than a syndicate that holds a similar piece of real estate that will have to be financed with a new, higher interest rate loan. The continuing low-interest rate, after all, would assure the new buyer (or buyers) a higher cash return on invested capital.[1]

Principal Amount of Loan

Although it is important to establish whether the syndicator has obtained financing that bears a favorable interest rate and amortization term, you should also take a long, hard look at the loan amount. It may be so large that the debt service, despite a low-interest rate and long amortization, may generate a negative cash flow.

It may be, of course, that the situation is deliberate. The

[1] The freely assumable loan is becoming increasingly common. Recent court decisions in some states have said that, under some circumstances, lenders cannot enforce due-on-sale clauses thereby making the loans assumable.

syndicator may have chosen to run a highly leveraged syndication in order to buy a valuable property for the smallest capital investment possible. Under these circumstances, you would maximize the tax write-offs you reap from the investment and you might look forward to a greater return on your investment. Nevertheless, you must remember that this highly leveraged property with its large loan and higher debt service will present you with increased risks. The risk may be particularly high during a recession or during periods when vacancy rates soar. Under these circumstances, if the investors are unwilling to contribute additional capital to fund operating deficits, there may be an especially quick slide to foreclosure.

EVALUATION FORMULAS

Loan Constants

So far we have considered the more important individual factors you should assess as you scrutinize the syndicator's financing arrangements. But it would be misleading and unrealistic to analyze each factor independently. How much weight, for example, should be given? How does any one factor change in different situations? Luckily, there are some formulas available that integrate the various financing factors and allow you to reach informed and balanced decisions.

One formula is known as the annual loan constant. It integrates interest rates and amortization terms to arrive at the annual loan payment for any given loan. To take an example, the annual loan constant for a 30-year, 9 percent loan, can mathematically be determined to be 0.966. Thus, if the loan amount is $1 million, the annual loan payments of interest and principal would be $96,600 ($1 million × 0.966). The lower the interest rate and/or the longer the amortization period, the lower the annual loan constant. Lower loan constants mean lower loan payments and therefore a larger net cash flow.

Why worry about loan constants? Because when you enter the real estate syndicate marketplace, you will find that different projects carry different financing arrangements. One building may have an 8 percent, 25-year loan. A second may have an 8.25 percent, 30-year loan. A third may have still other terms.

To compare the effect of the various provisions, you could sit down with reams of paper, a calculator, and a pot of coffee and engage in hours of calculations. Or, you could simply visit a title company or your local savings and loan institution, ask to look at their loan constant tables, and see which loan has the lowest loan constant.

Depending on the particular type of investment property you are evaluating, certain rules of thumb can be established to determine the acceptable parameters of the loan constant for any given type of investment. I would recommend your consulting with a real estate professional in whom you have confidence to assist you in determining acceptable loan constants for investments you are considering.

Debt Service-Gross Income Ratio

The loan constant can give you a clear picture of the impact of interest rates and amortization terms. But that formula does not leave room for the effects of gross annual income and loan amount on your investment.

To ascertain the combined effect and financial implications of interest rates, amortization terms, loan amount and gross income, you should turn to a formula known as the debt service-gross income ratio (or, more simply the debt service ratio). The ratio is computed by dividing the annual loan payments by annual gross income. It will tell you what percentage of gross income will go to servicing the debt, and what percentage is left over to cover expenses and to generate spendable cash.

If, for example, a rental property you are considering has an annual gross income of $100,000 and annual debt service of $55,000, the debt service ratio is 55 percent ($55,000/$100,000). That means that 45 percent of the gross income is available to cover other expenses (i.e., to make conventional repairs, replace fixtures, and cover vacancies), and for spendable cash. But, by adding up the potential costs[2] of running the property your syndicator wishes to purchase, you may determine that the potential expenses would require 46 or 47 percent of gross income. You would be warned, in other words, that a negative cash flow, or deficit, would be in the offering and that you

[2] Costs which, of course, you have determined independently.

might have to contribute additional capital to keep the syndicate solvent.

Different real estate investments, naturally, have different acceptable debt service ratios. Many real estate professionals believe that apartment buildings should have debt service ratios of less than 50 percent. According to this point of view, if the apartment building a syndicator is offering for investment has a debt service ratio greater than 50 percent, it would present you with a high degree of risk. In that case, you should look elsewhere, unless the building has other significant advantages that override its unfavorable debt service ratio.

Personally, I think that even a 50 percent debt service ratio can be too high and that you might be well advised to stay away from a building in which the debt service ratio exceeds 45 percent. You can see, for example, that if the expenses of running the property on a day-to-day basis are 45 percent and the debt service ratio is 50 percent, the syndicate will have only a thin 5 percent of annual gross income available for distributions from operations or to use should unforeseen contingencies arise.

In fact, if you are considering a syndicate with an office building, you should be especially conservative. In my opinion, you should not consider an office building with a debt service ratio higher than 40 to 42 percent. Office buildings have higher maintenance, repair, and utility costs than apartment buildings. Thus, since more of gross revenues must be allocated to these expenses, less is left for making mortgage payments.

Whatever debt service ratio you decide should serve as your frame of reference, be sure that you do not allow your feet to be set in concrete on the matter. A prospective investment may have a debt service ratio greater than the one you think is acceptable. However, I must emphasize that it does not mean that you should automatically discard the idea of participating in the syndicate. The debt service ratio could be reduced by making a larger cash down payment, thereby reducing the total loan amount.[3] When I run across an apartment building

[3] Increasing the down payment, naturally, has its disadvantages. It reduces the percentage of your tax write-offs, your equity buildup, and the appreciation of invested capital because those benefits remain constant. The ideal situation, of course, is one that has combined a highly leveraged transaction with a loan made with a low-interest rate, a long period of amortization, and therefore a low debt service ratio.

for which the debt service ratio is higher than the 45 percent I prefer, I, nevertheless, look at other factors: Whether the tenants are desirable, the amount of the property tax, whether the landlord or the tenants pay utility costs, the vacancy history, and, perhaps, most important whether there is room for increasing rents. Positive readings on one or on a combination of these factors can persuade me to go ahead even if the debt service ratio is higher than I prefer.

Whatever you decide is an acceptable debt service ratio, the formula will, at the very least, help you eliminate investments that have clearly unattractive financing. It can be used advantageously because debt service is a fixed amount, and can, therefore, provide a steady frame of reference, unlike property operational expenses that can fluctuate from year to year. Moreover, no other method of assessment provides you with an objective tool that so successfully combines interest rates, amortization periods, loan amounts, and gross annual income into a workable screening process.

Finally, it is interesting to note the interrelationship of the loan constant, the debt service ratio, and the desire to obtain as highly a leveraged transaction as possible. Consider the following general observations:

1. The lower the loan constant, the lower the debt service ratio; conversely, the greater the loan constant, the greater the debt service ratio.
2. The lower the debt service ratio, the more highly leveraged the transaction can be structured without incurring significant risk.
3. The greater the debt service ratio, the greater the risk of structuring a highly leveraged transaction.

HOW TO INCREASE PROFITS BY ELIMINATING HIDDEN RISKS OF FINANCING

Up to now we have discussed how interest rates, amortization periods, transferability provisions, and principal loan amounts can affect your potential profits from a syndicate investment. These are "up front" variables, easy to see, and, with the knowledge gained in this chapter, relatively easy to take into consideration when analyzing an investment. But, there are also hidden pitfalls that can affect your interest in an investment because the syndicate's financing may involve certain loan provisions, restrictions, and/or conditions that are not immediately apparent but can weigh heavily on the financial success of the venture.

Indefinite Loan Commitments

You should be especially careful to make sure that the syndicator has financing lined up when you are about to invest in a syndicate being organized around a new property.

As we discussed briefly in Chapter 2, new real estate projects generally are financed in two steps. First, the syndicator must obtain a temporary construction loan from a commercial bank in order to get the project off the ground. Second, in order to sustain the property once it is finished, he must have a permanent loan from a savings and loan institution or, in some cases, from a large insurance company.

Generally speaking, however, things are not that simple.

In many cases, before a commercial bank agrees to a construction loan, it will ask the syndicator to obtain, a commitment from a permanent lender that it will finance the project upon completion. In other words, the commercial bank is asking for a virtually ironclad guarantee that there will be money available to pay back its loan when construction is completed. If the syndicator is successful in his quest for an early commitment on a long-term loan the investors also have a strong guarantee that their project will be finished and that it will enter the real estate marketplace on a competitive basis. From your point of view, this is an ideal situation: No "hidden" risks here that the syndicator will have to give up the project midstream because no monies are forthcoming from a permanent lender.

There is, naturally, a catch. Because the permanent lender is committing itself to a substantial loan in the future, the rate it charges for this kind of a loan is generally much higher than the rates for more conventional real estate loans. As a result, the syndicator will use the commitment he received before ground was broken on the project only if other permanent financing under better terms cannot be found when the building is close to completion. Even if he does find a better permanent loan and does not use the earlier commitment, the syndicator must pay dearly for it.

Some commercial banks do make construction loans without asking the syndicator to obtain an early commitment from a permanent lender, especially during easy money periods. Even though it is a gamble, many developer-syndicators do prefer to go ahead on construction without having obtained some guarantees that a permanent loan will be available later. This saves the syndicator, and to some extent the investors, the increased costs that come with early permanent loan commitments.

Yet, when you consider a new property syndicate that has no permanent loan commitment from the very start, you are, to a great extent, operating in the dark. You have no way of knowing the amount of the permanent loan, the period of time over which it will be amortized, or the interest rate that will be charged. Without this vital information, you cannot make the calculations that will tell you what kind of cash return to expect on your investment. The syndicator may try to tell you that, based on recent events in the money market, you can be sure to expect a loan that will be amortized over, say 30 years, and will carry a 9 percent interest rate. But no matter what the syndicator says, you run the risk that between the time you make your investment and the time the syndicator finally obtains permanent financing, amortization periods have been shortened and interest rates may have risen substantially, reducing the anticipated financial benefits of your investment. Also, your syndicator may not obtain as large a loan as needed, which means that the syndicate investors will have to make up the difference.

Even more important, you are taking a chance that the syndicator may not obtain a permanent loan at all as the project nears completion. After all, the money market could dry up. Or, the syndicator's financial position may become unstable and lenders may shy away. Under these circumstances, it is quite possible that the commercial bank that made the construction loan would foreclose on the property. As a result, you would lose your entire investment.

To summarize, then, when you consider a new property, minimize the risks to your investment by making sure that, insofar as reasonable and possible, the syndicator has obtained an early commitment from a permanent lender. Your best guarantee is a firm early commitment that does not bear unreasonable costs. Only if other financial considerations make the syndicate attractive should you consider a project on which no permanent loan is in the offing when construction starts. The financing market is simply too precarious and arbitrary to gamble that everything will work out fine in the end.

Balloon Payments

Most properties are purchased with the aid of a second trust deed or some other form of secondary financing. These secondary loans, which are made for shorter terms than primary or first trust deed loans, generally require the purchaser of the property to pay only the interest (or very little principal) during the term of the loan. The purchaser pays off the principal in a large sum, or balloon payment, when the secondary loan matures.

This form of financing is advantageous because it increases the syndicate's (or any individual investor's) leverage in purchasing real estate. It allows the syndicate to use as little of its own capital as necessary to buy as big a piece of real estate as possible. At the same time, secondary financing can pose a tremendous financial burden on a syndicate because a few years down the road it will have to come up with the cash to meet the balloon payment.

Therefore, it is of great importance that you understand the full extent of the syndicator's secondary financial arrangements. First, be certain that the syndicator has not hidden or glossed over secondary financing arrangements. Second, if you find that secondary financing is to be used to purchase the property, be certain that the additional loan is not excessive or that the balloon payment will not come up too soon. There is no hard and fast rule, but I would say that you should be wary of a secondary loan that exceeds 20 percent of the purchase price.

Perhaps most important, you should make sure that the syndicator has made sound plans to meet the obligations imposed by the secondary loan. One way would be to arrange for secondary loan terms that call for payment of interest and principal. This, however, will reduce cash flow, which could create a greater risk than the balloon payment. The impact of a balloon payment can also be mitigated if the syndicator has drawn up a partnership agreement that calls for pro rata assessments on you and your fellow investors to build up a fund to meet the balloon payment. You might even try to secure a guarantee that the syndicator will advance the money for the balloon payment if need be.

The great majority of secondary loans, it must be said, are not settled by amortization or with the help of pro rata assessments or other existing funds. Usually, the owner of the property will simply refinance the first trust deed for a larger amount and use the proceeds to retire the second trust deed loan. This process entails risks. A property can usually be refinanced for a higher sum only if it has grown in value. The proceeds of the refinancing, after all, must be used to retire the primary loan first. Only if something is left over can the second loan obligation be met. Something will be left over only if the refinancing institution has appraised the property at a sufficiently high level to cover both obligations. I would suggest that you do not get involved in a property for which a balloon payment is due in less than seven or eight years. This will give the property a chance to increase in value.

Furthermore, in some instances a first trust deed cannot be refinanced because it carries a "lock-in" provision, a clause that specifically bars refinancing for a certain number of years. If your syndicate's second loan is due in five years and if the holder of the first loan will not allow refinancing for six years, the opportunity to meet the balloon payment in this fashion is closed.

Many syndicators arrange for secondary financing on the premise that the property will be sold before the balloon payment is due and that the proceeds of the sale will cover the secondary obligation. But don't forget that the syndicate's cash proceeds (and your cash return on capital) from the sale will be diminished by the amount of the balloon payment. Moreover, if the sale of the property calls for the new owner to assume the secondary loan obligation (that is, if it is not paid off with the proceeds of the sale), the buyer may choose to make a correspondingly smaller down payment since it is the buyer who will have to meet the balloon payment later.

The moral of the balloon payment story is simple. If adequate steps for retiring a secondary loan are not taken, you could lose your investment. I know of a syndicate that purchased an industrial building for $400,000. The syndicate made a $50,000 down payment, borrowed $250,000 on a first trust deed and $100,000 on a secondary loan. The terms for the second loan were simple. Payments for five years would be toward interest only. At the end of five years, the syndicate would have to make a balloon payment of $100,000 to pay back the principal. At the end of five years, the syndicate could not raise the required $100,000. The holder of the secondary loan—who. in this case, was the man who had sold the syndicate the property—foreclosed. The syndicate partners lost their entire investment.

Lock-in Loans

The lock-in loans we discussed above are usually made by large insurance companies. They are often sought out by syndicators because, unlike loans made by most savings and loan institutions, they can be transferred to a new purchaser; a great advantage if the loan carries an interest rate lower than those prevailing when the property is put back on the market.

But as many times as not that advantage is more than offset by the lock-in clause. The provision not only blocks refinancing of the first trust deed in order to meet a balloon payment, it also gets in the way of the syndicate's ability to sell its property for a maximum, immediate cash return.

A while back, for example, a Los Angeles syndicate bought an apartment building for $700,000 with a ten-year lock-in loan of $450,000. After five years, the principal had been brought down to $410,000. In the sixth year, the syndicate sold the property for $800,000. The buyer made a $160,000 down payment and assumed the $410,000 first trust deed loan. The syndicate had to make a $230,000 second trust deed loan for the balance of the purchase price. If the loan had not had a lock-in provision, the buyer could have obtained a new and larger first trust deed loan. The syndicate would then have received a substantially larger immediate cash return.

CONCLUDING COMMENT

Because loan payments usually constitute the largest expenditures on your syndicate investments, typically ranging anywhere from 40 to 60 percent of gross rentals, simple mathematics tells you that financing has the most direct and significant financial impact on your investment. For that reason, it behooves you to select syndicate investments that have not only competitive interest rates, amortization periods, and loan provisions, but also at the same time attempt to select investments with financing that does not have too many of the restrictive provisions and conditions discussed in this chapter. Once you have selected an investment with attractive financing, you are well on your way toward a profitable investment.

8

Real Estate Syndicate Projections—Or "Games Syndicators Play"

To look through the brochures some syndicators prepare for their potential investors is to look into a world where capital is safer than gold in Fort Knox, cash returns flow as steadily and bountifully as the waters of the Nile, and the potential for explosive appreciation is unmatched by anything short of a major oil find in your own backyard.

To an extent, the optimistic projections are understandable. Syndicators are selling a product. In order to move it, they present the assumed numbers and facts in the best light possible. Sometimes the syndicators do so because, plain and simple, they want to manipulate facts to their own advantage. Sometimes because, even if they are rigorously honest, they cannot be totally objective about the property they want to sell.

Under these circumstances, it is understandable that caveats (the tortured phraseology that tells you that "the above projections are considered accurate, but because various assumptions have been made as to future income and expenses, there can be no assurance of accuracy with respect to any of said projections") are often prescribed in small type and in out-of-the-way places in the brochure. What is *not* to be understood is that investors, who do not bother to read the fine print or who do not bother to scratch beneath the surface to check the facts put forth by the syndicator, nevertheless get angry when, at year's end, they receive a letter telling them that "due to unforeseen circumstances, actual operating results have fallen below those originally projected."

To spare yourself the agony of having to watch an investment ooze away, you should make every effort possible, especially when the syndicator promises particularly large rewards, to double-check the facts and figures on which the financial projections are made. True, a thorough investigation will be time consuming. But remember this: The time, money, and energy you will have to expend to try to salvage what remnants you can from a bad and injudicious investment will far outstrip whatever investigative efforts you make at the outset to guarantee that you are not being drawn into a losing proposition.

To help you evaluate a syndicator's projections, I have prepared the following checklist for you to follow:

1. Are the rental projections on target?

   If the syndicator has made an inadequate analysis of the rental market, if the rental market unexpectedly goes soft, and if extensive competition for tenants strikes an area, you can be sure that projected rental income will be affected. You can also be sure that rental projections for a new building are likely to be tenuous. Even a small error in projected rents will have a considerable adverse effect on the projected rate of return on your investment.

2. Has adequate allowance been made for maintenance and repair costs?

   Syndicators like to pretend they have invented the practically carefree property. Don't be fooled. It costs money to run a property well.

   Look at the building itself critically. Buildings that offer furnished units appeal to a clientele that is highly transient. The greater mobility factor will mean higher maintenance and repair costs. The same is true of residential or commercial buildings that offer month-to-month tenancies.

   Consider the age of the building. As a general rule, older properties require more maintenance, repair and replacement outlays than newer properties. Ask the syndicator if the property has been thoroughly inspected and what, if any, deferred maintenance costs are likely to crop up. For example, are hall carpets faded and due for replacement? Is the roof likely to leak this winter?

Buildings that rent to families will cost more to maintain and repair than buildings that cater to adults only. Be sure you know the tenancy of the syndicator's property before you take at face value the brochure's assurances about expected maintenance and repair costs.

Find out if the building is to be maintained by the syndicator's own crews (i.e., janitors, plumbers, etc., who may be a permanent part of the syndicator's staff), or if the building is to be serviced by outside contractors. Maintenance costs are likely to be lower if done by an in-house staff.

The size of the building, furthermore, will also influence maintenance and repair expenses. The costs of repairing and maintaining an elevator, Jacuzzi, sauna, security services, and recreational amenities should be fairly constant whether the building has 50 units or 25. But, the cost per *unit* and, therefore, the cost to you, is proportionately higher if you are investing in a building with a smaller number of units. Be sure, therefore, that you take this into consideration.

There is a similar difference between high-rent and low-rent properties. Because the cost of servicing high-rent buildings is a smaller percentage of gross rental income, maintenance costs can be said to be relatively lower. For example, the fee for servicing the pool in a 40-unit luxury building (let's say that each apartment rents for upward of $400) will be no more than the fee of servicing a pool in a unit that has 40 units that rent for $200 and up. But on the ledger, the cost of keeping the pool clean in the high-rent apartment is one half the cost in the low-rent building.

3. Have provisions been made for replacing amenities?

Carpets, drapes, and lobby furniture may have to be replaced during the years the syndicate holds the property.

Recreational equipment seems to be especially short-lived. If no allowance has been made for replacement costs, be wary.

4. Who pays for the utilities?

   Many furnished apartment buildings do not have separate utility meters for the tenants; that means the property owner pays for the utilities, an expense that is hard to pass on in the way of increased rents. Nor can you hope that utility expense can be kept down. Tenants, who do not feel they are paying for the energy bills, are not prone to take conservation measures.

   It is no less important to make an accurate estimate of utility costs in a new, unfurnished building where each tenant has a separate meter. The syndicate will still have to pay for the electricity to light common areas, for the energy it takes to run the laundry rooms, and to heat the pool or the sauna. Remember that utility costs are soaring and that the year-to-year increase may far outstrip the syndicator's estimates. Call your utility company and ask how much rates have jumped in recent years and what increases can be expected within the near future.

5. What is the vacancy factor?

   I have yet to see an offering circular that will project a vacancy factor greater than 5 percent, even though apartment and office buildings in many areas of the country suffer from far higher vacancy rates. You must make sure that the figure you are given is realistic. Check the vacancy factors of other buildings in the same area.

   When you study the vacancy factor, remember that an unrented unit will have a proportionately higher adverse affect on income in a building with few units than in a building with many.

   Keep in mind too that a poorly maintained and managed building will have more vacancies than a building kept in excellent shape. Thus, it may be important to find out how well (or poorly) the syndicator has maintained other properties.

Similarly, if you are about to invest in a building that is still under construction, check the track record of the architect and builder. Find out if other buildings they have designed and constructed have been well received by the public and have been filled quickly. In fact, I would even suggest that you ask for the addresses of their other buildings and that you take time out to make a personal inspection. The effort will help you assess whether or not the syndicator of a new property has judged its potential vacancy rate accurately.

6. Have property taxes been estimated properly?

Property taxes loom large on the debit side of any real estate investment. Thus, almost no other variable on the bottom of the balance sheet is likely to carry greater potential for torpedoing projected returns on your investment, especially if the syndicator has miscalculated how much will have to be paid into the governmental treasury. For example, a syndicator may have calculated that the $1 million property being offered is likely to bear a $30,000 yearly tax burden. But, it may turn out that he made a mistake, that the building is really assessed at $1.2 million and that the property tax for the following year will actually be $36,000, or roughly 20 percent more than anticipated. That $6,000 mistake may seem minor. But, if you and the other investors contributed $200,000, the miscalculation on taxes will mean that you get 3 percent less cash return on your investment every year.

To come to a more realistic estimate of potential property taxes (that is, a more realistic estimate than has been made by the syndicator), you should assume that there will be a new and higher assessment based on the price the syndicate is paying for the property. As a result, your estimate of projected taxes will be conservative; that is, on the high side. There will, accordingly, be no unpleasant surprises. You can follow a similar step in trying to determine property tax on a new project. Simply assume that the property's assessed value will be the same as the price the syndicate pays the builder and calculate the potential tax accordingly. Finally, check with the appropriate governmental offices and try to find out if there are plans afoot to reassess property in your area or to increase property tax rates.

7. Is the cost of servicing debt properly projected?

   Like property taxes, the cost of servicing the mortgage can be a significant variable in the investment. In fact, since it is the largest single expense factor in most investments, you should make sure that the syndicator has rendered an accurate account of the dollar and cents that will be needed to service the trust deed or mortgage. In an existing property, there is little risk that the mortgage payments will be erroneously stated because the loan terms are known. But, if the syndicator is offering a property that is still in the construction stage, chances are excellent that permanent financing has not yet been worked out. That means that you must consider the possibility that by the time the syndicator manages to arrange for permanent financing, interest rates may have risen. Thus, you and the other investors may have to bear debt service costs that are higher than those quoted in a brochure that the syndicator wrote up in earlier days when financing was cheaper.

8. Are records of past expenses and revenues available?

   If you are about to invest in an existing property, ask the syndicator to supply copies of records detailing the actual revenues and expenses for the property for at least the previous 12 months. The expenses and revenues projected by the syndicator in the offering should match the record fairly closely. Thus, if you find that the cost figures in the brochure are lower than those that show up in the records, you are in a good position to ask the syndicator to justify the discrepancy.

9. What is the syndicator's track record?

   An intense scrutiny of the facts and figures presented by the syndicator in the offering brochure will go a long way toward helping you make a wise decision about your investment. But, if you want to put your mind more at ease, look into the syndicator's past history and track record. Ask the syndicator to send you a letter (or some other written communication) that contains verifiable information about the syndicator's previous management efforts. Most important, request that the material that is supplied contains two very important figures about each project: The syndicator's projected rates of return, income and expense, and the actual benefits and expenses realized in each venture. The comparison will tell you whether the syndicator's present projections are accurate and reliable or whether the syndicator is doing some wishful thinking.

10. What do others think?

To round out your investigation, seek the advice of real estate professionals. Many property management firms, for example, have documented statistical studies of what various operating expenses should be for different kinds of property. That information will be invaluable when you analyze the syndicator's projections.

To give you an idea of how your evaluation process should work, I have outlined below a typical apartment building investment. The syndicator's claims are presented and analyzed.

OFFERING CIRCULAR—VILLA VICENTE APARTMENTS, LTD.

Property Description

Villa Vicente Apartments, Ltd., is a California limited partnership, being formed to purchase a 55-unit furnished apartment building of Spanish motif, located in Los Angeles, California. The building is presently under construction and is expected to be completed by June 30, 1978, approximately four months after its acquisition by the partnership. The individual apartment units will be attractively furnished, featuring color coordinated carpets, appliances, and furnishings. There will also be extensive recreational facilities, including a swimming pool, Jacuzzi, sauna, and a paddleball court.

TABLE 4

Projected Annual Income and Expenses

	1978	*1979*	*1980*
Income	$60,000	$200,000	$220,000
Less 5% vacancy	—	10,000	11,000
Effective gross income	$60,000	$190,000	$209,000
Operating Expenses:			
Property taxes	10,000	35,000	38,000
Resident manager	3,000	6,000	6,000
Professional management fee	—	—	10,450
Utilities	8,250	16,500	17,500
Gardener	400	800	800
Maintenance and repairs	2,400	8,000	9,000
Insurance	1,500	1,500	1,600
Elevator	300	700	800
Pool	300	700	800
Rubbish collection	300	800	850
Total Expenses	$26,450	$ 70,000	$ 85,800
Net before debt service	$33,550	$120,000	$123,200
Less: Trust deed payments	$51,000	$102,000	$102,000
Spendable Cash Flow	($17,450)	$ 18,000	$ 21,200
Spendable Cash Flow as percent of Investment	(5.7%)	5.88%	6.92%

Notes:

1. The projections contained herein are predictions of future events and are, therefore, by their very nature, subject to error or change.
2. The 1978 projections are for the six-month period from June 30, 1978 through December 31, 1978. The $10,000 in property taxes represents the December 1978 installment.
3. Rental income is projected as follows:

35 one-bedroom units at $275 (including utilities) = $9,625 × 12	$115,500
20 two-bedroom units at $350 (including utilities) = $7,000 × 12	$ 84,000
	$199,500
Laundry income (coin machines)	500
Total Gross Annual Income	$200,000

4. Total invested capital is $306,000.
5. Management fees are prepaid through 1979.

ANALYSIS

Like other optimists in the syndication field, this syndicator assumes that the vacancy factor in the building will hover at a low 5 percent.

But let's assume that the syndicator is not that far off but that, nevertheless, the projected 1979 rents are a mere 5 percent off. But a 5 percent error, it turns out, is no pittance for it will effectively reduce net spendable cash by $9,500.

Projected 1979 gross income	$190,000
5% error	×0.05
Decrease in gross income	9,500
Projected 1979 spendable cash	18,000
Gross income that is not forthcoming	9,500
Actual spendable cash	$ 8,500

Thus a 5 percent error in projected rents escalates into more than a 50 percent reduction in spendable cash.

You should, therefore, be careful when you study the figures given you about projected rentals for a new building. For example, note in the above example that the building is not scheduled for completion until mid-1978. Calculation will show that monthly rentals during the last half of 1978 must average $10,000 to meet the syndicator's projection that the rental income by year's end will total $60,000. This means that in the first six months of business, the building will have to have an average occupancy rate of 60 percent. Any investor considering this building must decide whether the rental market in the area is strong enough to ensure that a sufficient number of tenants will be found to meet the syndicator's target. If the market proves to be weak, the syndicate investors will have to bear the extra costs during the first year of operation.

According to the syndicator's figures, the maintenance and repair costs for the building will be about 4 percent of gross annual income. This seems low, especially for a furnished building. A more realistic maintenance and repair expense factor for the Villa Vicente apartment is closer to 6–8 percent of gross income; that is, $12,000 to $16,000 rather than the syndicator's wishful $8,000.

Furthermore, if you study the fact sheet carefully, you'll see that the syndicator has made no provisions for replacements of nonstructural parts of the building. True, not much may have to be replaced in a building during the first year or two of its existence. But if the syndicate holds onto the building for three or four years, costs to replace furniture, carpeting, drapes, Ping-Pong and pool tables (among other things) are likely to build up. At least 2 percent of gross income should be allowed.

Anything more than a superficial reading of the syndicator's brochure also shows that the utility expenses for the investment are underestimated. In this building there are no separate meters for each tenant. Thus, it is the owner that will be footing the entire utility bill. And, as I said before, it would be difficult to pass utility costs on to tenants in the form of increased rents. It will be difficult to encourage the tenants to save energy since they do not feel that they have a direct stake in the utility costs.

Experience too would show that an estimated allowance of $25 a month for utilities for each unit should be made. For the building mentioned above, this would mean $16,500 a year. Furthermore, in a 55-unit building, common area (i.e., hallways) utility costs would easily add another $6,000 a year. Finally, we see the syndicator has projected a 6 percent yearly increase in utility costs. However, recently utility costs have been increasing as much as 25 percent a year.

Look closely through the fact sheet. Do you see any provisions for legal fees, accounting fees, business license fees, or supplies? Or for payroll taxes or workman's compensation for the resident manager? All of these costs could add $2,000 to $3,000 to the operating cost of the syndicate property.

Revised Projections

Let us now compute the probable understatements in the projected operating expenses for 1979 for the above investment, which is the first full year of operations for the property. For the sake of simplicity, let's assume that projected rental income and the vacancy factor are accurate. The probable minimum *understatement* of expenses is as follows:

Utilities	$ 6,000*
Legal, accounting, payroll taxes, worker's compensation insurance, business license	2,000
Maintenance and repairs	4,000†
Replacements	4,000‡
Total Understated Expenses	$16,000

* $16,500 + $6,000 = $22,500 as compared to the projected $16,500.

† 0.06 × $200,000 = $12,000 versus projected 0.04 × $200,000 = $8,000.

‡ 0.02 × $200,000 = $4,000.

Thus, it would appear that only $2,000 of cash flow can realistically be expected in 1979, rather than the projected $18,000.

CONCLUSION

The bottom line on most syndicate investments is net cash flow. Net cash flow governs your investment yield, determines, to a large extent, your investment's market value, and strongly affects your investment risk. You should, therefore, never accept a syndicator's projections of revenues and expenses without personal investigation. Before you deliver your check to the syndicator, if you want to make sure you're investing in what you think you are, you must take the time and make the effort to thoroughly investigate and evaluate each significant item of projected expense and revenue in the syndicator's investment brochure.

9

Tax Concepts and Benefits of Real Estate Syndicates

Not too long ago, a physician who had invested in a real estate syndicate came to me to seek some advice. Three years earlier, he had joined a syndicate with a $50,000 contribution. Now, he had received news that the syndicate's project was in deep trouble and that he and his fellow investors would each have to ante up $10,000 a year for the next four years to try to salvage the situation. Should he commit himself to pay the additional sum, he wanted to know.

The puzzled doctor had brought the syndicator's original offering and some partnership tax returns for me to look over. Even a cursory review of the materials convinced me that the project was—and always had been—doomed.

"I would cut bait," I told him. "I would not invest an additional $40,000 in this."

"But then I'll lose everything," he wailed.

"Well, all I can tell you is better $50,000 than $90,000. There is no way this building can be turned around. You should never have invested in the first place. What made you do it?"

"Because the tax write-offs looked so great."

Because the tax write-offs looked so great. A theme that has echoed and re-echoed thousands of times in the offices of attorneys who are consulted by unhappy investors.

Therefore, before we get into a discussion of the tax benefits that can come with a syndicate investment—and, to be sure, the tax benefits can be sizable—let me issue one clear-cut warning. You should keep it firmly in mind:

> **Never invest in a real estate syndicate just because it offers bountiful tax benefits. Given an alligator-infested swamp, any sharp syndicator can turn it into a tax deduction for you. Therefore, you should always analyze a prospective investment only on its economic merits. Only if you have decided that a project will yield economic returns should you then analyze and take into consideration the investment's tax benefits. Tax benefits are the frosting on the cake. They are not the cake.**

The Benefits of Tax Shelter

Most tax shelter investments, including real estate, have considerable financial benefits.

Although tax shelter investments do not eliminate the payment of income taxes, they do allow you to defer the payment of income taxes to a later date. The deferral of taxes has significant economic value. It allows you to use money that would otherwise be paid to the government to generate additional income.

If you look ahead and plan well, you can make subsequent investments to generate the tax deductions you will need to offset the income that you will have to declare when investments made in earlier years are sold.

In other words, that day when you will finally have to pay taxes can be postponed again and again. When you finally do have to recognize the income, you will probably be in a lower tax bracket because you have retired or because you are declaring it in a year when income from other sources is small.

Finally, inflation makes the deferral of taxes become particularly important. Tax dollars paid at a later date are "cheaper" than the tax dollars you would have had to pay had you not taken advantage of a shelter.

Tax shelter investments also enable you to receive all, or a portion, of operational cash flow without income recognition.

Tax shelters also enable you to convert what would otherwise be ordinary income into capital gains income. Capital gains, of course, are taxed at a lower tax rate. Thus, you have deferral of income and the conversion of ordinary income to capital gains.

IMPORTANT TAX SHELTER CONCEPTS

Nonrecourse Loans

With limited exceptions, real estate partnerships are the only investment partnerships that can write off more than 100 percent of their invested capital. They can do so because under the law they are allowed to benefit from nonrecourse loans; that is, mortgage or trust deed loans that allow a lender to foreclose against a property in case of default but not to move against the borrowing partnership or any of its members to make up any deficiency between the amount loaned and the amount recovered in a foreclosure sale.

Nonrecourse loans entitle syndicate investors in limited partnerships to increase the tax basis of their partnership interests by their pro rata portion of such loans. To illustrate, assume that ten investors each contribute $10,000 to a partnership. The proceeds are used to make a $100,000 down payment on a $500,000 apartment building. The $400,000 balance of the purchase price is obtained with a typical nonrecourse first trust deed or mortgage. The tax basis of each investor's partnership interest is equal to $10,000 (cash contribution) plus 10 percent (their profit interest in the partnership) times the amount of the nonrecourse loan ($400,000). Therefore, each investor's initial tax basis is $10,000 + $40,000, or $50,000. This means that each investor may take up to $50,000 in tax deductions. Thus, conceivably, the investor could deduct 500 percent of the actual $10,000 cash investment. I don't want to leave you with the impression that these deductions are *automatic*. Remember always that deductions can be taken only if the investment is generating sufficient operating losses, depreciation write-offs, and so on. It also means that any distributions of operational cash flow will not be taxed as long as the cash distributions do not exceed the tax basis of the investor's partnership interest. Therein lies one of the major inherent tax benefits of real estate syndicate investments.

It is important to remember that if the mortgage, or trust deed loan, in the above example, had been made as a "recourse" or personal liability loan, the tax basis of each partner would be only $10,000. In most cases, they would not be entitled to more than $10,000 in tax write-offs and/or nontaxable cash distributions during the investment term. Thus, although the investment property itself may generate more than $100,000 in tax losses and cash flow, these benefits could not be utilized by the investors.

Consequently, it is of paramount importance that you make sure that your syndicate is using nonrecourse financing if you expect to take full advantage of the tax write-offs and cash distributions from the syndicate investment. There are various tax structuring methods used by syndicators to obtain nonrecourse financing. The major one is the use of the so-called all-inclusive trust deed (AITD) or "wraparound" mortgage.

The All-Inclusive Trust Deed

The AITD can significantly leverage your tax write-offs. It also can create significant investment risks, if not properly structured, or improperly used.

An all-inclusive trust deed is a trust deed that is subordinate to, and all-inclusive of, one or more underlying senior deeds of trust (usually the existing bank loan). It is also a purchase money trust deed that, therefore, is a nonrecourse obligation in many states. For that reason, it substantially increases the tax basis of the partnership interests of the investors, thereby enabling them to leverage their tax write-offs from the investment.

To illustrate the concept of the AITD, let's compare a conventional financing transaction with one involving an AITD. Assume that the syndicate buys a building for $100,000 by making a $20,000 down payment, by assuming the seller's 6 percent bank recourse first trust deed loan of $60,000, and by obtaining a new $20,000, 8 percent interest, second trust deed from the seller. This may be illustrated as follows:

Price	$100,000
Down payment	−20,000
Balance of purchase price	$ 80,000
First trust deed—bank	−60,000
Second trust deed to seller	$ 20,000

The buyer thus makes trust deed payments directly to the bank on the first trust deed loan and directly to the seller on the second trust deed loan.

But in an AITD agreement arrangement, your syndicate would not assume the seller's first trust deed. Rather, the seller will keep the $60,000 mortgage or first trust deed loan. Then, the seller will make a new, personal loan to the syndicate of $80,000 at 8 percent. In other words, the new loan "wraps around and includes" the existing first trust deed loan of $60,000. As a result, the syndicate would make all its monthly payments to the seller. The seller would then make the appropriate payments to the bank for the original first trust deed and keep the rest. The figures look like this:

Price	$100,000
Down payment	−20,000
AITD	$ 80,000

Now, you might ask, what is the advantage of this complicated purchase structure? For the buyer, it can have the following benefits:

1. The AITD syndicate loan is usually nonrecourse as opposed to the $60,000 bank loan which is not and, therefore, increases the tax basis of the partnership interests of the investors by $80,000, rather than only $20,000 (conventional second trust deed) on the conventional purchase structure. Thus, conceivably, the potential tax write-offs available to the investors have been increased 400 percent.

2. In some states, the all-inclusive structure can be used to preserve favorable interest rates on the underlying trust deed loans because the trust deed holders cannot accelerate the loans or increase the interest rates.

3. In some states, the underlying trust deed holders cannot charge the buyer transfer fees or assumption fees on AITD

transactions, as they can on conventional loan assumption transactions.

4. Since the AITD is a new obligation, it can be structured, in terms of principal and interest amortization schedules, to the needs of the particular property.

The seller may also find important financial benefits in the use of the AITD such as:

a. In the conventional case above, the seller will only earn $1,600 interest a year on his $20,000, 8 percent interest, second trust deed. But, look what happens in the all-inclusive structure. The seller receives annual interest of $6,400 (0.08 × $80,000), from which only $3,600 ($60,000 × 0.06) must be paid to the first trust deed holder. The seller, thus, makes a net annual profit of $2,800 just on the interest differential. This is a 14 percent yield on the $20,000 equity in the all-inclusive note ($80,000 − $60,000).

b. The seller can also use the all-inclusive structure to take advantage of an installment sale that will significantly defer taxable income on the sale of the property and will entitle the seller to receive more cash in the year of sale without violating the installment sale requirement that a seller cannot receive more than 30 percent of the contract price in cash in the year of sale.

c. Since an AITD transaction preserves the interest rate on the underlying trust deeds, in the event the seller has to foreclose on the AITD because of a default by the buyer, the seller will be able to take back the property with the same interest rate on the underlying trust deed. On a conventional sale, however, if the buyer assumed the underlying trust deeds, the lender probably would insist on an increase in interest rate on its trust deed, and a subsequent foreclosure by the seller would require the seller to take back the property subject to the higher interest trust deed.

All-Inclusive Checklist

Because of the importance and potential for abuse of AITDs, you should always analyze their structures carefully. The following checklist should assist you in your analysis:

1. Make sure a collection or escrow account has been set up by the syndicator and seller for the payment of the all-inclusive note and the underlying note. In other words, you want to be certain that once the seller receives the monthly payments on the AITD, the corresponding payments to the first trust deed holder will be made, and that the seller won't merely be pocketing the money.
2. Make sure that the equity buildup in the AITD is at least equal to the equity buildup in the underlying trust deeds. If it isn't, the equity of the seller in the AITD will actually increase over time and you could have an unexpected balloon payment.
3. Make sure that the means for paying off the AITD has been specified so that you won't have problems when the property is resold. Also, inquire whether the AITD is freely assumable and whether it may be prepaid without penalty.
4. If the seller of the property is the syndicator, or an entity related to the syndicator, make sure the syndicator discloses *all* personal profits realized on the AITD.
5. If prepaid interest is paid on the AITD, make sure that appropriate credits are included in the amortization schedule of the AITD note.
6. In many cases, a lender will insist that a new buyer (in this case the syndicate discussed above) assumes or guarantees the first trust deed loan. Since this is a recourse loan, which does not increase the tax basis of the investors' partnership interests, some syndicators will try to work around the problem by creating a nonrecourse all-inclusive loan on top of the first trust deed.

   In theory, the syndicate now owes $140,000 (above example) on a $100,000 property. However, both the seller and the buyer understand that the AITD is a fiction. However, so does the IRS who will not accept the AITD. Therefore, you must make sure that the syndicate is not assuming or guaranteeing the first trust deed loan.
7. Make sure the AITD amount is greater than the amount of the underlying deeds of trust. If it is not, the seller will have no equity in the AITD, and the IRS will attack the AITD as a shame instrument.

Depreciation as a Source of Tax Benefits

Most of the tax benefits that accrue to the syndicate investor are generated through the depreciation of the building or buildings, the so-called improvements on the land. Although depreciation methods can become quite complex, the basic principle behind the concept is fairly simple. According to the Internal Revenue Service Code, a building, like any other capital good in any business, deteriorates year by year, even though there is no physical evidence that the decline is in progress. Since, according to this fiction, the syndicate is losing slowly the very thing that is central to its business, the syndicate has a right to write off, against revenues, the cost of the improvements.

The basis of the depreciation concept is another accounting and tax fiction, the estimated useful life of the building. Estimated useful life does not mean the length of time the building is likely to stand before it is hopelessly outdated or crumbles into dust. Rather, estimated useful life is the period of time over which the building (or any other business asset, for that matter), is expected to be useful to the taxpayer while the taxpayer uses it in a trade or business or in the production of income. That means that while a building may reasonably be expected to last 100 years, its estimated useful life is much shorter. Typically, for tax purposes, a building's estimated useful life will vary from 25 to 40 years.

It should also be noted that a building's major components may be depreciated separately since they, quite naturally, can be expected to have different useful lives. For example, carpets, drapes, and appliances have considerably shorter useful lives than the actual structure. As we will see, the greater the share of the purchase price that can be allocated to components with short useful lives, the greater the depreciation tax benefits will be.

There are several different ways in which buildings and their components can be depreciated. The simplest method is called straight-line depreciation. This means that the cost of the building (and components) less their estimated salvage value, are deductible in equal amounts over the estimated useful life of the building. Thus, for example, if a $200,000 building has an estimated useful life of 20 years, $10,000 ($200,000/20) may be depreciated, or expensed, each year.

Buildings may also be depreciated by the "declining balance" method. This procedure is one of the so-called accelerated depreciation methods because it provides greater depreciation deductions in the early years of the investment and smaller ones in the latter years. The declining method is used to generate higher tax losses in the earlier years of the investment. The declining balance method cannot exceed twice the appropriate straight-line rate and is applied in each year to the unrecovered, or undepreciated cost of the particular asset. Specifically, new residential buildings, such as apartment buildings, are entitled to take 200 percent of the straight-line amount. However, used residential buildings are entitled to take only 125 percent of the straight-line amount if their estimated useful lives are at least 20 years. New commercial properties, such as office buildings and shopping centers, are entitled to 150 percent of the straight-line amount. Used commercial properties may only take straight-line depreciation.

To illustrate the declining balance method, let us assume again that a building costs $200,000 and has an estimated useful life of 20 years. Under straight-line depreciation, the maximum that could be depreciated is, as we have said, $10,000 per year, or 5 percent of the cost of the asset. If, however, the building is a new apartment complex, the 200 percent declining balance method could be utilized. This would mean that the syndicate could depreciate 10 percent of the undepreciated cost each year. Thus, in the first year, $20,000 could be depreciated (0.10 × $200,000). In the second year, the 10 percent would be applied to the undepreciated cost, or $180,000 ($200,000 – $20,000), resulting in a second-year depreciation of $18,000, and so on. Although the method is an accelerated one, the amount of depreciation declines each year and, at some calculated point in time, the annual amount of depreciation will be less than the straight-line amount.

Another form of accelerated depreciation is the "sum-of-the-year's-digits" method. In the "sum" calculations, depreciation allowance is apportioned at a rate measured by the number of years remaining in the estimated useful life, divided by the sum of all the years' digits in the useful life of the property. Thus, an asset with an estimated useful life of five years would have a depreciation factor for the first year equal to 5/15 $(15 = 5 + 4 + 3 + 2 + 1)$. In the second year, depreciation would be 4/15, and so on. Thus, a $100,000 depreciable asset, having a useful life of five years, would result in a first-year depreciation allowance of $100,000 × 5/15 or $33,333. As you can see, the shorter the useful life of the depreciable asset, the greater the annual depreciation and the greater the tax benefit.

Because there are so many variables in real estate investments, the syndicator (or usually the syndicator's accountant) determines which specific method of depreciation to use and what kind of an estimated useful life span to assign the syndicate's project. When you consider an investment, you must also decide whether the syndicator's chosen depreciation route fits your needs. However, you should also make certain that there is sound justification for the depreciation allowances taken by the syndicator. When component depreciation is being calculated, the IRS insists that the actual costs be used as the basis for depreciation in new properties. If you are investing in an older property, the IRS says, depreciation calculations must be based on an appraiser's estimates of the costs of replacing the building's various components.

The Tax Benefits of Depreciation

The benefits of financial leverage extend to depreciation. Although investors put up only a fraction of the purchase price of a building, they are entitled to depreciate the *full* cost of the building.

How do these depreciation tax deductions help you? Depreciation tax deductions are used first to offset net income generated by the property. If there is enough depreciation left over, it is used to offset any personal or business income you receive from sources other than the syndicate investment. To illustrate, let's take a look at the following investment situation: An office building, purchased for $1.2 million, has a useful life of 30 years. The price includes $900,000 for the building and $300,000 for the land.

Gross annual rental income	$175,000
Less: Annual operating expenses	$ 85,000
	$ 90,000
Less: Annual loan payments (interest only)	$ 80,000
Net Annual Cash Flow	$ 10,000
Less: Annual depreciation (straight-line method $900,000/30)	$ 30,000
Net Annual Tax Loss	$(20,000)

Each year, the investors will receive the $10,000 cash flow, even though, for tax purposes, the investment shows an operating loss of $20,000. Moreover, the cash distributions to the investors will be tax free. Further, the investors may use the $20,000 of tax losses to offset any other income they might have.

Depreciation Recapture

As indicated at the outset of this chapter, tax shelters allow you to defer payment of taxes on income, but do not eliminate taxes forever. For example, if you have a $500,000 depreciable asset in which $100,000 of depreciation has been taken during its first five years of use, the tax basis of that asset is reduced to $400,000. If the asset is then sold for $500,000, taxes will have to be paid on the amount of $100,000 ($500,000 – $400,000), even though no cash may have been received from the sale. Thus, while there were previous paper losses, now you may be faced with the problem of paying taxes on paper profits.

However, when straight-line depreciation is used, the total profit earned on the sale of the property is treated as capital gains income. Therefore, it is subject to a considerably lower tax rate. Thus, depreciation has served to defer taxes and to convert profit that would otherwise be ordinary income into capital gains income.

Under accelerated methods of depreciations, however, that portion of the depreciation taken in excess of the amount that would have been allowed under the straight-line method (in other words, the accelerated portion), is treated as ordinary income,[1] rather than as capital gains. This is commonly referred to as depreciation recapture.

Capital Gains Benefits

Favorable capital gains treatment has long been an appealing feature of real estate investments. There are, however, certain limitations you should keep in mind in your individual tax planning. The taxpayer has the choice of either excluding one half of the *excess* of net long-term capital gains over net short-term capital losses, or paying an alternate 25 percent tax on the first $50,000 of the *excess*. Thereafter, the effective tax rate on all long-term capital gains will increase up to a maximum of 35 percent (one half the 70 percent maximum rate on unearned income). Further, as will be discussed, the effective rate may be even further increased as a result of the 15 percent minimum tax on the 50 percent portion of the capital gains which was excluded from income. Thus, careless tax planning can result in a high tax rate for even capital gains.

Proper tax planning, however, will enable you to maximize the capital gains benefits of real estate investments. For example, in the year the syndicate is reselling its property, you may wish to retain some or all of your appreciated individually owned capital assets in that year so that you may take advantage of the 25 percent alternate tax to the fullest extent. Alternatively, you could sell individually owned capital assets that have declined in value to reduce the net long-term capital gains. Further, since the capital gains from the sale of the syndicate property may use up or even exceed the exemption from the minimum tax, you may wish to forego other real estate investments that year which utilize accelerated depreciation.

Investment Tax Credit Benefits

Certain items of depreciable personal property, such as elevators and washing machines, purchased by syndicates entitle the investor to an investment tax credit. Presently, the

---

[1] As required in the provisions of the 1976 Tax Reform Act.

maximum credit is 10 percent of the cost of eligible property which has a useful life of at least seven years. A lesser credit is available for qualified property whose useful life is at least three years. This maximum investment credit, however, is only available for property which is acquired and placed in service before January 1, 1981. Thereafter, the maximum credit allowable to each investor is $25,000 of his or her federal income tax liability for the taxable year plus 50 percent of the tax liability in excess of $25,000. For example, if an investor's tax liability is $50,000, the maximum credit would be calculated as follows: $25,000 + 0.50 (50,000 – 25,000) = 25,000 + $12,500 = $37,500 maximum credit. If however, a sale of the eligible property occurs within seven years from the date of acquisition, the investor would incur a tax liability resulting from the recapture of part or all of the investment credit previously taken.

THE TAX BITE ON PROFITS—WHAT HAPPENS WHEN YOU SELL

I must stress that you should be very careful when considering the tax benefits projected by a syndicator, especially if the syndicator is also talking big about all the profits that are to be realized when the property is resold. Many syndicators simply fail to tell you (and, in fact, to recognize themselves) about the tax burdens that a sale is likely to generate. Unless your syndicator knows the IRS ropes, you may very well make a good profit, only to find the IRS ready and waiting for a large share of the money that was going to buy you that new 60-foot sloop.

To illustrate the tax consequences of a sale, let's assume that six years ago you invested $25,000 in a syndicate that raised $250,000 to purchase a new 40-unit apartment building for $1 million. The $250,000 was used to make a cash down payment. The rest, $750,000, was obtained through a first trust deed loan. Let's assume further that the property was just resold for $1.3 million, and the buyers made a $300,000 cash down payment. The syndicate, however, extended the new purchasers a $325,000, five-year second trust deed. According to the syndicate's accountant, the adjusted tax basis for the property (purchase price less past depreciation) is $500,000. Your syndicate's first trust deed loan balance now stands at $675,000.

To calculate the taxable income from the sale of property, you must compare the amount realized, that is, the net sales price, with the adjusted tax basis of the property. In our example, this would be calculated as follows:

Sale price....................	$1,300,000
Less: Adjusted tax basis........	500,000
Taxable income...............	$ 800,000

Matters might have been all right if your syndicate had indeed received $800,000 in cash. But it didn't. It only received $300,000 cash. A substantial part of the sale profits—$325,000—is in the form of a loan that will not be collected for five years. In other words, the syndicate will have to pay taxes on $800,000 in the year of the sale, even though it has received less than half that amount.

The day of reckoning has thus come a-thundering. Not only will you not realize the great profits promised, but chances are that you may even have to dig into your pocket to pay the taxes on your share of the profits that do come in this year.

How could this disaster have been avoided?

First, you might have insisted that the syndicator structure the sale on an installment basis, which, according to tax law, can be carried out only if the syndicate accepts 30 percent or less of the sale price in the first year. In any case, a proper installment sale would have enabled the syndicate—and by extension you as an individual investor—to spread the $800,000 taxable gain over the term of the second trust deed; that is, over five years.

As the proposed sale is presently structured, it would not qualify as an installment sale. Why? Because the difference between the mortgage still outstanding and the adjusted tax basis of the property is deemed to be cash received in the year of the sale. In your case, for example, the syndicate received a $300,000 cash down payment. But the mortgage loan amount is $675,000 and the tax basis is $500,000, and the difference of $175,000 is considered cash received by the IRS. Thus, as far as the IRS is concerned, the syndicate received $475,000 more than the allowed 30 percent of the $1.3 million sale price.

Under these circumstances, the syndicate would not be allowed to claim the benefits of an installment sale. A smaller cash down payment would avoid the problem.

The syndicate would be able to take advantage of installment sales provisions if it were to use an all-inclusive trust deed or contract of sale to dispose of its property. In fact, I believe that an all-inclusive trust deed or contract of sale in which the syndicate is loaning the buyer the entire difference between the down payment and the sale price is preferable. By using an all-inclusive trust deed, the buyer doesn't assume the original mortgage. Therefore, the tax code does not require that the difference between the mortgage and the adjusted tax basis be considered cash received in the year of sale. Thus, the $300,000 down payment now represents only 23 percent of the total sales price and this is well within the requirements of an installment sale exemption. Moreover, not all of the $300,000 received is treated as taxable income. By IRS standards, that amount can be broken down into taxable income for the year and into nontaxable return on capital. The taxable income is calculated by first determining the so-called gross profit percentage. This is done by dividing gross profit, or $800,000, by the sales price of $1.3 million. In this case, the percentage turns out to be 61.5 percent. Accordingly, the amount of income subject to taxes in the year of the sale is 61.5 percent × $300,000, or $184,500. Finally, the $615,500 of taxable income which represents the balance of the total profit will be spread out over the five years of the all-inclusive trust deed and will, therefore, be subject to less severe taxation.

Summarizing then: You should not, in most instances, approve any sale of a syndicate property unless it has been structured as an installment sale. You should also insist that the syndicator give you considerable advance notice of the contemplated sale so that you will have enough time to make additional tax-sheltered investments or to take other steps to minimize your tax burden.

Foreclosure Sales

A foreclosure is a painful matter. However, the tax consequences of foreclosures can make the process disastrous. The Internal Revenue Code treats a foreclosure sale, for tax purposes, the same as any other sale of property. Let's say that you invested \$20,000 in a syndicate formed to develop a new federally assisted housing project at a cost of \$1 million. The project was financed with \$200,000 of investor capital and a first trust deed loan of \$800,000. After five years, operating expenses, maintenance, repairs, and replacements had escalated so much that the syndicate could no longer make the mortgage and tax payments. As a result, the bank foreclosed on the property. Finally, let's assume that over the five years, the syndicate had taken \$400,000 in accelerated depreciation deductions and that at the date of foreclosure the unpaid loan balance was \$750,000.

What are the tax consequences of the foreclosure sale? First, of course, you have lost your original \$20,000. But to add insult to injury, you will have to report \$7,500 of ordinary income and \$7,500 of capital gains income on your individual return. Why? Follow the mathematics:

Sales price	\$750,000*
Less: Undepreciated cost basis	600,000†
Total Taxable Income	\$150,000
Excess portion recaptured as ordinary income	\$ 75,000‡
Individual portion (0.10 × \$75,000)	\$ 7,500
Straight-line portion recaptured as capital gains	\$ 75,000
Individual portion (0.10 × 75,000)	7,500

* Under the tax laws the amount of the unpaid loan remaining at the time of the foreclosure sale is treated as proceeds of sale, since the partnership is relieved of this liability.

† Computed \$1 million cost, less \$400,000 depreciation.

‡ Assumes that the 200 percent double declining balance method of depreciation was utilized, in which case the accelerated portion (50 percent) of the depreciation recapture is treated as ordinary income, and the straight-line portion (50 percent) of the depreciation recapture is treated as capital gains.

A Special Matter—Federal Assistance Programs

Investments undertaken in conjunction with federal assistance programs (see Chapter 2) receive much more favorable tax treatment than conventional property investments—to induce private capital to enter the field, perhaps to compensate investors for the risks they are taking when they venture into these programs.

A federally subsidized property receives special treatment when depreciation recapture is calculated. The amount of accelerated depreciation that would otherwise be subject to recapture as ordinary income is reduced by 1 percent a month for each month the property is held by the syndicate beyond 100 months. In other words, if a syndicate were to hold a federal assistance program apartment building for 200 months, all of the recaptured income would be treated as capital gains. Under the 1976 Tax Reform Act, conventional real estate investments must recapture all of the accelerated depreciation as ordinary income.

There are other tax advantages to be garnered in a federal assistance program. Since these programs provide federal funds for up to 90 percent of the required financing, a syndicate must invest only 10 percent of its funds to obtain the property. The resultant leverage further increases the percentage tax write-offs on investment capital to which the investors are entitled. Unlike conventional properties, until 1982, new properties built with federal subsidies will give syndicate investors the right to deduct all construction interest and property taxes. Finally, projects being rehabilitated under FHA-236 subsidized rehabilitation programs give investors the chance to depreciate the rehabilitation expenditures over a short five-year period. However, to qualify for this favorable tax treatment, rehabilitation expenditures must exceed $3,000 per dwelling unit over a period of two consecutive years. No more than $20,000 can be spent on each unit. Whatever the sum spent, the rapid depreciation results in substantially greater tax write-offs for the investor than any other type of real estate venture. Rehabilitation projects, you should note, are subject to periodic congressional review. Don't count on taking advantage of their tax benefits until your accountant or lawyer has confirmed that the rehabilitation program provisions are still in effect.

The Tax Reform Act of 1976

The Tax Reform Act of 1976 imposed important restrictions on tax shelter investments. However, of all possible tax shelter investments, real estate has been affected the least. As a result, real estate investments still provide substantially greater tax benefits than any other form of investment available today. For example, in most other forms of tax shelter investments, investors are limited on the amount of tax deductions they can take; that is, according to the new laws, investors in most ventures can deduct only what they have "at risk." They can deduct no more than the amount of capital they have invested. But in real estate investments, it is still possible for investors to deduct considerably more than they have invested.

But while the Tax Reform Act has treated real estate less severely, it has not left the field totally unscathed. There have been changes of which you should be aware.

Construction Period Interest and Taxes

One of the more significant tax changes affecting real estate investments is the new requirement that construction period interest and taxes be capitalized and amortized over a stated period. Prior to 1976, such expenses could be deducted in full in the taxable year when paid. In 1982, a full ten-year amortization period will be applied to commercial properties, and in 1984 to residential properties, such as apartment buildings. Until 1982 and 1984, the 1976 act provides for phase-in of such deductions. The phase-in is outlined in Table 5.

TABLE 5

Year Paid	*Percent Deductible in Year Paid for Residential*	*Percent Amortized Equally over Following Years for Residential*	*Percent Deductible in Year Paid for Commercial*	*Percent Amortized Equally over Following Years for Commercial*
1976.......	100%	0%	50%	50%
1977.......	100	0	20	80
1978.......	25	75	16.67	83.33
1979.......	20	80	14.29	85.71
1980.......	16.67	83.33	12.50	87.50
1981.......	14.29	85.71	11.11	88.89
1982.......	12.50	87.50	10	90
1983.......	11.11	88.89	10	90
1984.......	10	90	10	90

Notes:

1. The amortization period commences at the latter of the year following the year the expenses were paid or accrued, or in the year when the property is first placed in service, such as commencement of occupancy of the property.

2. The phase-in for federal low-income housing projects does not commence until 1982, and therefore all construction period interest and taxes on these properties are fully deductible in the year when paid until 1982.

Prepaid Interest and Loan Fees

Prior to the Tax Reform Act of 1976, prepaid interest deductions were offered by many real estate syndications. Prepaid interest deductions, when properly structured, provided substantial tax deductions in the year of purchase of the property. Thus, much of the initial investor capital contributions could be deducted in the year of the investment by allocating it toward prepaid interest on a mortgage or trust deed. The same was true with respect to loan points, or loan fees. There has been much litigation and IRS pronouncements in recent years concerning the validity of prepaid interest and loan fee deductions, and the courts have generally restricted the use of such deductions.

However, the 1976 Tax Reform Act has ended prepaid interest deductions. Therefore, one of the major tax benefits of all tax shelter investments has been eliminated. Loan fees can still be deducted, but must now be amortized over the term of the loan (except for loan fees paid in connection with the purchase of personal residences, which may still be deducted in the year paid).

Allocations of Income and Losses among Partners

Syndicate partnership agreements frequently provide for the allocation of profits and losses disproportionately to the capital contributions of the investors. Thus, some syndicate partnership agreements provide for the allocation of tax losses to certain partners and the allocation of cash distributions to other partners. This enables tax- and income-oriented investors to join together in the same investment.

However, the 1976 Tax Reform Act has imposed certain restrictions on such special allocations. The general rule remains that the allocation of overall income or loss can be designated by the partnership agreement even though the allocation may be disproportionate to the capital contributions of the partners. The new Act, however, now requires that the partners receiving the special allocations be able to demonstrate that the allocations have substantial economic effect. That an investor is not just trying to avoid taxes and is pursuing a clean-cut business purpose may meet the "substantial economic effect" requirement. Because further clarification of this new provision must await court decisions, it would be prudent if you had your lawyer or accountant review a partnership agreement that provides for allocations disproportionate to investor capital contributions.

The 1976 Tax Reform Act also prohibits retroactive allocations of income or loss. Thus, an investor, when selling a partnership interest to another, may not agree to allocate tax losses incurred prior to the transfer to the incoming partner. All tax losses and income must now be prorated according to the portion of the year in which the buying partner was a partner. In addition, an investor who obtains a partnership interest after the property has been purchased may no longer be allocated any tax benefits that arose prior to entry into the partnership.

Other Deductions

Over the years, syndicators have attempted to devise other tax structuring methods in an effort to deduct certain cash payments, such as consulting fees and prepaid management fees. The Internal Revenue Service and the courts have almost uniformly rejected such tax deductions. These items, the rulings have said, must be capitalized. You should view with suspicion any promise that such fees will be deductible. Rather than providing additional tax deductions, these attempted tax write-offs often result in Internal Revenue tax audits.

In general, prior to the enactment of the 1976 Tax Reform Act, syndication and organization fees were sometimes deducted by syndicates. The 1976 Tax Reform Act states that organizational syndicate costs, such as legal and accounting fees, are not fully deductible in the year when paid. Such costs may, however, be capitalized and amortized for a period of not less than five years. However, syndication fees, such as those related to the issuing and marketing of syndicate interests in the partnership, are not subject to this amortization provision. These fees must be capitalized, rather than expensed, and they may not be amortized over any period of time.

10

How to Analyze the Tax Aspects of Your Syndicate Investment

While it is useful for you to have some understanding of the principles and theories that support tax benefits offered by real estate syndicates, ultimately you must determine if the specific benefits are compatible with your own personal financial planning and objectives.

Your personal tax needs will depend on such things as the nature and amount of your present income, anticipated future sources of income, estate planning desires, and your age. These things must be considered in analyzing whether the tax consequences of particular syndicate investments are beneficial to you. You must consider, for example, the tax shelter's impact on such personal tax considerations as the following:

a. The minimum tax on tax preference items.
b. Tax preference items and the maximum tax on earned income.
c. Investment interest restrictions.
d. State income tax.

In order to assist you in integrating the nature and type of tax deductions arising from real estate syndicate investments with your own personal tax situation, the individual tax considerations are discussed below.

MINIMUM TAX ON TAX PREFERENCE ITEMS

The 1976 Tax Reform Act imposes a 15 percent minimum tax on "tax preference" items in excess of $10,000, or one half of the taxpayer's regular tax liability, whichever is greater.

Tax preference items include excess depreciation over the straight-line amount, one half of capital gains, and itemized deductions (other than medical and casualty deductions) in excess of 60 percent of your adjusted gross income.

To illustrate the application of the minimum tax on tax preference items, assume that you have capital gains of $40,000, and excess depreciation of $20,000, from your real estate investments in a certain year.

Tax Preference Items	
$20,000 (40,000 capital gains × 0.50) +	
$20,000 (excess depreciation)	$40,000
Less: Annual exclusion	10,000
	$30,000
Minimum tax rate	×0.15
Extra taxes payable	$ 4,500

Thus, if you knew you were going to have capital gains of $40,000, it may have been better for you to have invested in real estate syndicates that year that did not utilize accelerated depreciation. In fact, whenever you expect your tax preference items to exceed the greater of $10,000 or one half of your regular tax liability in any year, you must consider the minimum tax consequences of the real estate investments you are considering for that year.

TAX PREFERENCES AND EARNED INCOME

Earned income, such as wages and professional fees, are subject to a maximum tax rate of 50 percent, whereas unearned income (dividends, interest income, and so on) is subject to a maximum tax rate of 70 percent. Under the 1976 Tax Reform Act, each dollar of tax preference items reduces the taxable income eligible for maximum tax treatment by a like amount. The net effect of such reduction is that tax preference deductions, such as excess depreciation, generate a maximum tax savings at a 50 percent rate, rather than a 70 percent rate. Therefore, your personal income tax bracket and the nature of your income, will determine how beneficial accelerated depreciation is for you.

To illustrate, assume that you have $200,000 of earned income, $100,000 of unearned income, and $40,000 of tax preference items. Assume further that you invest in a real estate tax shelter that is taking accelerated depreciation. The effective rate of tax savings applicable to the tax preference accelerated depreciation is as follows:

	Rate (percent)
Deduction shelters unearned income	70%
Deduction shifts earned income from 50% to 70% bracket	(20)
Effective Deduction Rate	50%

EXCESS INVESTMENT INTEREST LIMITATION

"Excess" investment interest is the excess of investment interest expenses over investment income for the taxable year. One form of investment interest is interest on indebtedness utilized to purchase or hold property for investment purposes, such as trust deed interest payments on investment real property. An important type of investment income is rental income.

Under the 1976 Tax Reform Act, you may only deduct on your personal tax return investment interest equal to $10,000 plus the amount of investment income. You may, however, carry over unused investment interest expenses to subsequent years.

To illustrate the effect of this provision, assume that you pay $50,000 in investment interest and have $20,000 of net investment income. Your interest deduction is computed as follows:

Base amount allowable	$10,000
Investment income	20,000
Allowable investment interest deduction	$30,000
Interest disallowed	$20,000*

*The amount disallowed may be carried over to subsequent years, subject, however, to the same restrictions.

In the context of real estate syndications, the relevant determination is whether the property is considered investment property or business property. Within this context, real property held for rent is generally considered the conduct of a business and, therefore, the interest expense limitation does not apply because it would not be considered investment interest. However, in net lease syndications, the property is considered as investment property and, therefore, the interest limitation does apply. Whenever the syndicate is guaranteed a specific cash return or is guaranteed in whole or part against loss of income, it will be considered by the IRS to be a net lease situation. Accordingly, when investing in net lease syndications, such as sale leasebacks, or syndications containing cash flow guarantees, you must be aware of the possible limitations on interest expense deductions.

STATE INCOME TAX CONSIDERATIONS

Most investors consider only the federal income tax consequences of prospective investments. Because of increasing state income tax rates in most states, you must also consider whether your state of residence will allow equivalent deductions on your state income tax returns. Many states do not allow equivalent deductions for certain types of tax write-offs.

TAX SHELTER ANALYSIS CHECKLIST

To help you analyze and evaluate the tax benefits of prospective syndicate investments, I have prepared the following checklist:

1. Make very sure that the syndicate will be treated as a partnership for income tax purposes, or you will not be entitled to use the partnership's tax losses on your individual tax returns. This is perhaps the major tax consideration of any syndicate investment. In recent years, the Internal Revenue Service has attempted to classify limited partnerships as corporations for tax purposes, so that the limited partners would not receive the anticipated tax benefits of their investment.[1] There has been considerable litigation in this rapidly evolving tax area,

[1] This is particularly true when the syndicator-general partner is a corporation.

as well as important Internal Revenue Service rulings. Although the current trend of court decisions has been in favor of investors, many syndicators obtain independent tax opinions from tax attorneys concerning this issue because of its fundamental tax importance to investors. If no tax opinion has been obtained, then it would be advisable for your attorney to review the partnership agreement to determine whether its structure and provisions will enable it to be treated as a partnership for tax purposes.

2. Look more closely at the nature and quality of a syndicate's tax deductions than at the amount of tax deductions. Don't be diverted by numbers. It is important to know, for example, what the Internal Revenue Service's current policy is with respect to the particular types of tax deductions involved in your investment. For example, depreciation deductions usually are more likely to withstand IRS scrutiny than prepaid management fees and other front-end deductions because the IRS has always questioned the legitimacy of such deductions. Your tax accountant or attorney should be able to advise you of current IRS tax policy with respect to the various types of tax deductions.
3. Inquire whether a favorable IRS ruling has been obtained covering the major tax benefit offerings of the syndication. This is, perhaps, your best assurance of the tax worthiness of the tax issues in question. Unfortunately, however, such rulings are costly and time consuming, and are therefore, usually obtained only by the large publicly registered syndications.
4. If no IRS ruling has been obtained, inquire whether an independent tax attorney has given a written opinion as to the tax consequences of the investment. A favorable tax opinion is also a reflection on the tax worthiness of the investment. Once again, however, such opinions are usually expensive and many syndicators do not obtain them.
5. Find out whether the syndicator's previous syndications have been audited by the IRS and, if so, inquire how they fared against Internal Revenue Service scrutiny. This

should provide you with a good indication of the syndicator's tax structuring competence, and of the likelihood the deductions would be upheld in an audit.

6. Make sure all tax assumptions are appropriately conservative. For example, determine whether reasonable "useful lives" have been used for depreciation purposes. Or whether reasonable allocations have been made between land and improvements for depreciation purposes. Find out the factual basis for the allocations. Since the amount of first-year depreciation deductions will depend on how long your syndicate has owned the property in that year, it is important to determine whether the syndicator can realistically manage to raise the capital needed to buy the property by the scheduled closing date. If the syndicator fails to meet the projected date, you will not gain all the benefits you expect. Since depreciation may not be taken on new construction until it is completed, make sure the projected completion date is realistic. You should ask the syndicator to provide you with the reasons and documentation of the underlying tax assumptions.
7. Be skeptical of tax deductions based on payments to the syndicator, especially if the deductions are not supported by a tax opinion. Examples include prepaid management fees, rent-up fees, organizational fees, and undocumented consulting service fees. The use of such deductions are usually red flags to the IRS. The IRS will usually insist that they be capitalized, rather than expensed. Prepaid expenses, in particular, have regularly been rejected by the IRS.
8. If accelerated depreciation is to be used, make sure the syndicate is the "first user" of the property. If the seller or builder collects rents and allows tenant occupancy prior to the close of escrow, it is the seller or builder and not the syndicate, who will be the first user of the property. Consequently, the syndicate will not be entitled to utilize accelerated depreciation.
9. Make sure that not more than 49 percent of the partnership interests can be resold within a 12-month period. If more than 49 percent are sold the partnership will be "terminated" for tax purposes, and that can have signifi-

cant adverse tax consequences. For example, the partnership would no longer be considered the "first user" of the property, but rather the "second user." Further, the partnership assets will be deemed distributed to the investors, and if the basis of the assets exceeds the basis of the investors' partnership interests, the excess will be taxable income to the investors.

10. Closely scrutinize tax shelters with substantial first-year tax write-offs. The Internal Revenue Service and the courts have consistently disallowed tax deductions which result in a "material distortion" of income to the syndicate partnership. In other words, if in the first year of the investment, there is little or no gross income, which usually occurs in year-end syndications, there is a risk that the Internal Revenue Service will contend that there was a material distortion of income and thereby reject the tax deductions in their entirety.
11. Whenever investor guarantees or net leases are involved, be aware of potential excess investment interest limitations that may preclude you from utilizing all the projected tax write-offs.
12. Whenever the syndicator is projecting tax losses in excess of your cash investment over the term of the investment, you must make sure that nonrecourse financing has been utilized so that the tax basis of your partnership interest will be increased to allow you to utilize the projected tax losses. Otherwise, you cannot avail yourself of all the projected write-offs.

To provide you practice in analyzing the tax worthiness of prospective investments, set forth below are excerpts from a tax-structured syndicate investment, followed by an evaluation analysis of the projected tax write-offs.

OFFERING CIRCULAR—SAN LUIS APARTMENTS, LTD.

Property Description

San Luis Apartments, Ltd., is a California limited partnership, being formed to purchase a 50-unit furnished apartment building of Early California motif, located in San Luis Obispo, California. The building is presently under construction and is expected to be completed by June 30, 1978, which is approximately four months after its acquisition by the partnership. The individual apartment units will be attractively furnished, featuring color coordinated carpets, appliances, and furnishings. There will also be extensive recreational facilities, including a swimming pool, Jacuzzi, sauna, and paddleball court.

Investment Objectives

The primary objective of this investment is tax shelter. It is also expected that there will be cash flow from the investment and equity buildup from the mortgage principal reduction. During the first calendar year, it is expected that 52.7 percent of investors' initial capital investment will be tax deductible.

Terms of Purchase

The purchase price of the apartment building is $1.3 million with a down payment of $190,000 and the balance of the purchase price represented by an all-inclusive trust deed (AITD) of $1,110,000 in favor of the seller-builder. The AITD bears interest at 8.5 percent, has annual payments of principal and interest of $102,000, and will be subordinate to a 30-year existing first trust deed of $1 million that has annual payments of principal and interest of $90,000.

Partnership Capitalization

A total of $306,000 of limited partnership interests will be sold, in minimum units of $10,000. A contribution of $6,000 per unit must be made on or before March 1, 1978 and $4,000 per unit on or before July 30, 1978.

Allocation of Funds

Investor capital contributions will be allocated and applied as follows:

Cash down payment	$190,000
Construction interest and property taxes	50,000
Loan fees	20,000
Two years' prepaid management fees	20,000
Organizational expenses	3,000
Legal and accounting	3,000
Working capital and reserves	20,000
Total	$306,000

Projected Tax Losses

	1978	*1979*	*1980*
Net Income before Debt Service	$ 33,450	$ 120,000	$ 124,000
Less:			
Loan fees	(20,000)		
Construction interest and taxes	(50,000)		
Prepaid management fees	(20,000)		
Annual interest	(46,750)	(93,500)	(92,000)
Annual depreciation	(58,000)	(110,000)	(100,000)
Total Projected Tax Loss	$(161,300)	$ (83,500)	$ (68,000)
Tax savings for investors in 50% tax bracket	$ 80,650	$ 41,750	$ 34,000
As a Percent of Investment	26.4%	13.6%	11.1%

Notes:

1. The various Internal Revenue Code provisions, regulations promulgated thereunder, the interpretation thereof by the Treasury Department and the courts are necessary subject to change from time to time. Therefore, nothing contained herein shall constitute any representation with respect to the tax aspects involved in this investment. Prospective investors are advised to consult with their attorney or accountant concerning the tax consequences of this investment as it affects them.

2. Depreciation has been calculated on the basis of the 200 percent declining balance method, using a 25-year useful life for the building shell and varying shorter useful lives for the building's components, such as carpets, appliances, and fixtures. The projections assume a building completion date of June 30, 1978.

TAX ANALYSIS

Since the syndication's prime objective is to maximize tax losses, this already suggests that the syndicator's tax assumptions may be liberally, rather than conservatively, oriented. Therefore, it is prudent to analyze the basis for each item of purported tax write-offs. For example, the syndicator is using a 25-year useful life for depreciation of the building shell. This is too short a useful life for this type of investment for several reasons: First, new apartment buildings have an economically useful life of more than 25 years. In addition, since the lender made a 30-year loan on the apartment building, there is independent evidence that the useful life is more than 25 years. Moreover, since the syndicator is also using component depreciation for furniture, appliances and fixtures, and so on, the building shell, itself, should have a longer useful life, probably 40 years. Accordingly, it is probable that the Internal Revenue Service would contest the useful life of the building shell.

With regard to component depreciation, you should inquire as to the basis for the syndicator's allocation to the various components, as well as the useful lives utilized. Since new construction is involved, actual cost figures should be utilized in the allocations. Any allocations at variance with actual cost is suspect. In cases of used properties, in the absence of actual cost data, there should be an independent reproduction cost appraisal supporting the component allocation.

The syndicator has not provided the allocation of the purchase price to land and improvements. You should request this information. If the allocation to land is less than the property tax allocation, the IRS could reject the allocation, unless there is valuation data that supports the allocation.

Since projected depreciation deductions are based on a completion date of June 30, 1978, you must determine how realistic that date really is. Any delay in completion will reduce the projected tax write-off for 1978. Accordingly, you should find out whether the syndicator has included potential delays due to the winter rainy season, whether any labor strikes are anticipated, and whether there are any current material shortages.

The syndicator intends to deduct two years' management fees in advance. This has commonly been used by syndicators to increase first-year tax write-offs. However, the Internal Revenue Service has regularly rejected such write-offs, contending they are not ordinary and necessary business expenses. The Internal Revenue Service will not allow, as a current deduction, any payment for services that are to be performed after the end of the partnership's current tax year. Moreover, such an item is a red flag for an Internal Revenue Service audit of the partnership.

There appears to be an error in the syndicator's calculation of construction interest and property taxes. Under the 1976

Tax Reform Act, these items are fully deductible only through 1977 on conventional apartment buildings. Taxes and construction interest accrued or paid in 1978 would only be 25 percent deductible in 1978, and the balance would be amortized over three years beginning with the *later* of the following year (1979) or the year when the property is first placed in service (i.e., rented). Accordingly, the projected 1978 construction interest and property taxes of $50,000 for the above investment would be only $12,500 deductible in 1978, with the remaining $37,500 deductible in 1979, 1980, and 1981, respectively.

There may be another problem with respect to the construction interest, however, because of the fact that the interest appears to be payable on a construction loan, which is not the syndicate's obligation. In order for interest to be deductible, it must be paid on a valid debt of the taxpayer. Accordingly, if the construction loan is the obligation of the builder, then the partnership cannot obtain a tax deduction for interest payments made on it.

There is also insufficient information with regard to the payment of loan fees. Once again, if the fees relate to a construction loan, which is not the obligation of the syndicate, no deduction will be allowed by the syndicate. If, however, the fees are paid on the AITD, there is a better chance for deducting them. However, even here, it should be noted that the 1976 Tax Reform Act requires that loan fees on investment properties be amortized over the term of the loan. Therefore, in no event will the $20,000 in loan fees be all currently deductible by the syndicate in 1978, as projected by the syndicator.

Note that the projections are based on a 50 percent tax bracket taxpayer. If your tax bracket is less than that, the projected tax benefits would be reduced accordingly.

Don't forget to consider the effect of the investment's tax structure on your individual tax planning. For example, the fact that accelerated depreciation will be utilized can have a two-prong effect on your personal tax situation. First, the excess portion of the depreciation is a tax preference item and will, therefore, increase the amount of items subject to the 15 percent minimum tax imposed by the 1976 Tax Reform

Act. Second, the amount of excess depreciation reduces, dollar for dollar, the amount of earned income subject to the maximum 50 percent tax. Because of these considerations, you should probably consult your accountant to determine the amount of additional taxes you may have to pay as a result of the excess depreciation.

ALL-INCLUSIVE TRUST DEED ANALYSIS

You should find out the difference in principal reduction, or equity buildup, between the first trust deed and the all-inclusive trust deed. The amortization schedules are sometimes structured so that the first trust deed builds up equity quicker than the AITD. As a result, the seller's equity in the AITD, or residual profit, will become larger over the term of the loan, and you may find yourself with an unexpected large balloon payment later on. A skillful syndicator will insist that the equity buildup in the AITD at least equals that of the first trust deed.

You should make sure that neither the syndicator nor the partnership has assumed the first trust deed loan. As you will recall, this would allow the Internal Revenue Service to nullify the AITD as a sham and thereby limit your total tax write-off to only the amount of your invested capital.

You should also make sure that an escrow or collection account has been established to assure the timely payment of both the AITD and the underlying first trust deed.

11

The Partnership Agreement: If You Have Seen One, Have You Seen Them All?

Legal documents, especially those that demand a personal signature, elicit an almost comical response from people. Show even the most intelligent man or woman a piece of paper that sports a "wherein" or a "wherefore" and the person will:

1. Read the first two paragraphs very seriously.
2. Allow an annoyed look to creep onto his or her face.
3. Start to scan, at an increasingly fast pace, succeeding paragraphs and pages.
4. Say "Uh-hu."
5. Sign on the line where the small "X" appears.

Perhaps the legal profession is at fault. We have been criticized—and justifiably so—for drafting documents in tortured, convoluted, and out-of-date English. Nevertheless, there is no excuse for not reading a legal document that will have a major impact on your life. This is especially true of the document that will serve as the Constitution and Bill of Rights of your syndicate investment: the Limited Partnership Agreement is the document that limits your liability in the investment and it is this agreement that establishes, or should establish, the rights, benefits, and obligations of the syndicator, who is the general partner, and the investors, who are the limited partners.

I want to state clearly right here at the beginning that all too often investors get into trouble because they have not read the partnership agreement, or have not read it carefully enough. And, not knowing what is in the agreement, the investors neglect to impose proper restrictions on the powers and authority of the syndicator. Almost always, the irate investor who rushes into a lawyer's office demanding redress because a syndicator has just done something seemingly outrageous, discovers that the syndicator's action, as abusive and excessive as it might have been, was no more or no less than what was permitted by the partnership agreement.

Therefore, whether you are about to make your first or your tenth syndicate investment, I suggest that you obtain a copy of the partnership agreement, take it home, and, after properly girding yourself, sit down and read it word for word. In the pages that follow, I will discuss the more important provisions that should be included in the partnership agreement to provide your investment with adequate safeguards.

LIMITED LIABILITY

One of the most attractive features of syndicate investments is precisely the limited liability that comes as part of the deal. The syndicator or general partner acts as the business agent for the limited partners. In that role, the syndicator makes arrangements for the repairing, refurbishing, maintaining, selling, and so on, the property. But in the course of doing business, nothing the syndicator does, says, or signs makes the investors liable to third-party creditors. Thus, as a general rule, investors are assured that, even if the investment goes sour, they will not be liable for anything beyond their capital contributions to the partnership. In other words, banks, consultants, property managers, and suppliers who might be left in the lurch by the downfall of a syndicate and its property have no recourse against the individual investors.

However, limited liability is conferred only if the syndicator has filed a certificate of limited partnership with the recorder's office in the county where the partnership has its principal place of business and in the county where the real estate to be syndicated is situated. While the recorded certificate gives the limited liability legal sanctions, it also gives the syndicate the legal right to hold property in its name. Finally, the recorded certificate serves to give all potential creditors public notice that the syndicate is conducting business as a limited partnership, opens to their inspection the partnership's capital structure, and outlines the nature of the rights and obligations of the limited partners and the general partner.

The certificate of limited partnership may be a part of the partnership agreement itself or, it may be a separate document, giving in abbreviated form, all relevant data about the partnership. In any event, you should always insist that the syndicator give you a certified copy of the *recorded* certificate of limited partnership as soon as possible. Only that will assure you that you do have limited liability. I know syndicators who have neglected to record certificates—or have recorded them too late—and have, as a result, exposed their investors to personal liability to creditors.

A recorded certificate, however, is not an absolute guarantee against liability. You may still be personally liable to the syndicate's creditors if you participate in the management or control of the partnership's business. For example, if you are given the right to approve certain business transactions or expenditures, you are in effect participating in the business of the partnership. You may then be personally liable to the creditors of the partnership. There are several statutory exceptions to this rule contained in the Uniform Limited Partnership Act (which has been adopted by most states) :

1. Limited partners may vote on the election or removal of a general partner.
2. Limited partners may vote on the termination of the limited partnership.
3. Limited partners may vote on an amendment to the Partnership Agreement.
4. Limited partners may vote on the sale of all, or substantially all, of the assets of the partnership.

Even though these specific acts may involve participation in the partnership's business, they will not lead to personal liability for you. Be sure that the limited partnership agreement you sign does not give you rights to participate in the syndicate's business beyond the four exceptions outlined above.

Limited partners are, however, personally liable for unpaid contributions which they have agreed to make to the partnership. Thus, if the partnership is structured so that investors have to contribute a specified amount of money each year for a certain period of time, they are liable to creditors for the full amount of those agreed-upon contributions. Thus, you should make sure you know the maximum amount of capital you will be required to contribute during the term of the partnership. You should also make sure that the partnership agreement contains a provision that no further capital contributions shall be required of the limited partners beyond those expressly provided by the partnership agreement.

Finally, if you receive cash distributions when your partnership is being dissolved or during the investment period, you will have to return that money if there are unmet obligations to creditors.

FUTURE ASSESSMENTS

Many limited partnership agreements give the general partner the right to request additional capital contributions from investors if more money is required to keep the partnership solvent. These provisions include penalties in the event an investor fails to contribute more capital. You should closely scrutinize provisions that call for additional assessments. You want to make sure that you are not opening yourself up to endless demands for money. Furthermore, remember that investors are still liable for unpaid contributions they originally agreed to make. Thus, these assessment provisions modify the limited liability character of your partnership.

Assessment provisions are prevalent in syndicates that deal in unimproved and nonincome producing real estate such as citrus groves or recreational land. The assessments are generally needed to cover the carrying costs of the properties during the investment period; that is, until the properties are, hopefully, developed or resold. The inherent risk in these syndications is that some investors may be financially unstable and unable to meet their assessment obligations. Or, they may simply refuse to pay the additional monies when due. As a result, the burden of carrying the property falls on the shoulders of the remaining partners. If they, in turn, cannot carry their assessments and those not met by reluctant investors, the property may have to be sold at a substantial loss, or worse, it may even be lost through foreclosure.

The risk to you is increased if you belong to a syndicate that has a large number of investors who do not know each other. In such syndications it is quite difficult to organize in time to take effective protective measures, and as a result the property may be foreclosed before any protective action can be implemented.

If you are going to invest in syndications that may call for additional contributions, you should make sure that the syndication is structured to minimize the risk of defaults. For example, the partnership agreement should provide that you receive immediate notice of any investor default. It should also require that each investor have a high net worth. The agreement should also require that the syndicator be required to raise enough capital to provide large cash contingency reserves.

PROVISIONS FOR SAFEGUARDING INVESTOR FUNDS

It is important that the partnership agreement spell out a mechanism or procedure to ensure that investor capital will be safe. Under the partnership agreement, the syndicator should be required to deposit individual capital contributions into a trust fund until all the money is raised. Without such a provision, funds can be misappropriated all too easily.

Furthermore, the partnership agreement should also forbid the syndicator from using any investor funds until all the capital needed to launch the project is raised. For example, a syndicator may intend to raise $80,000 to make a down payment on a building, $20,000 to improve it, and $10,000 to keep in reserve for emergencies. If the syndicator is tempted—and allowed to—to use the first $80,000 to make the down payment and close escrow on the building, the money already contributed and hastily used would be jeopardized if the syndicator were then to fail in efforts to raise the additional $30,000 needed.

The partnership agreement should also specify clearly how the investor funds will be used. If there are no restrictions on the use of funds, the syndicator could raise money ostensibly to buy one property but then use the funds to buy another piece of real estate, without investor approval. At best, that other property may not meet your investment criteria. At worst, it may represent a direct risk to your money.

The partnership agreement should also define the amount of time the syndicator will be permitted to raise the required capital. Naturally, this provision should also state that your funds must be returned immediately if the syndicator fails to meet the deadline. For example, let's assume that a syndicator is attempting to raise $200,000 to acquire an apartment building by June 15 of this year. If you are one of the first investors, you must make sure that all the money will be raised in time for the property to be purchased by the 15th so that you can benefit by the tax write-offs provided by the investment. Thus, the partnership agreement should state that if the funds are not raised by, let's say, June 1, your own money will be immediately returned to you so that you can find an alternative investment.

PROVISIONS FOR THE SYNDICATOR'S COMPENSATION

From the syndicator's point of view, the partnership agreement has one important section—the one that outlines the fees to be paid for services rendered.

That section, however, is important to you also. It is essential that the clauses that outline how much the syndicator is to receive be clearly and precisely written. You want to make sure that there is no ambiguity and that there is no room for unpleasant surprises later. The partnership agreement is a contractual document and under it the syndicator is legally entitled only to that compensation spelled out within its pages.

REMOVING THE GENERAL PARTNER

The partnership agreement should outline the circumstances and procedures under which the syndicator can be removed and replaced. Many agreements do not have removal provisions and the investors sometimes find they are stuck with a syndicator they feel is incompetent or not conscientious.

KEEPING THE GENERAL PARTNER

Conversely, the partnership agreement should also restrict the syndicator's right to retire or resign as a general partner. After all, many investors—you included—participate in a particular syndicate only because they trust the syndicator. The partnership agreement should also restrict the syndicator's right to sell or assign to others any financial interest the syndicator has in the investment.

BOOKS AND RECORDS

Most partnership agreements require the syndicator to maintain accurate records and books of account. However, while these are open for your inspection, the information they contain usually does not tell you much about the gains (or losses) your investment is making—unless you want to pay your own accountant to review them.

The agreement should require the syndicator to provide you (at least semiannually) with a detailed status report about the investment. You should be told about vacancies, rental rates, competitive conditions, required improvements and repairs, current problems, and other relevant information. The status report may help you detect negative trends and, perhaps, avoid unpleasant surprises later on. For example, the report may show you and other investors that the syndicator is mismanaging the property. As a result, you may have the ammunition you need to fire the syndicator should you wish to do so.

If the partnership agreement does not set up a mechanism for meetings with the syndicator, it is a good idea to insist that the general partner meet on a regular basis with the investors. The meetings will allow you to ask questions directly and to meet and get to know the other investors. Unity among the limited partners can be a strong incentive to the syndicator to do better, or at least not to do ill.

TRANSFER OF PARTNERSHIP INTERESTS

At one time or another you may want to sell your interest in an investment. Or, perhaps, you may want to buy the partnership interest an investor has in another syndicate.

A sound partnership agreement should outline the procedures for transferring your investment interest. To protect the person to whom you sell your interest and to protect you if you buy someone else's interest, the partnership agreement should provide that a purchaser of an existing partnership interest may become a "substituted limited partner," entitled to all the same rights as the original investor. Furthermore, it is necessary to be sure that the syndicator has recorded an amendment to the certificate of limited partnership in the county recorder's office, reflecting the transfer—again to put creditors on legal notice. If the amendment is not recorded, the purchaser of an existing syndicate investment will have no legal right to inspect the partnership books and records and will not have the right to vote on any of the issues open to an investor "referendum."

There are certain risks you may run if you become involved in a transfer of partnership interests. According to the Uniform Limited Partnership Act, the seller of a partnership interest is not relieved from any liability that exists for unpaid contributions. For example, a partnership agreement may call for an initial investment of $10,000 and an additional contribution of $5,000 later. If you sell your partnership interest before the additional contribution is due, you are not totally released from your obligation. If the person who bought your syndicate interest agrees to make the second contribution but then defaults, you will still be required to dig into your pocket for the additional $5,000.

Similarly, if you buy someone else's partnership interest, you will be "buying" the seller's liabilities as well. There is one exception. You are not held responsible for liabilities of which you had no knowledge at the time you acquired the interest because the liabilities were in some way withheld from you. That means, however, that you cannot absolve yourself from liabilities whose existence you could have ascertained. Thus, in the example above, if you were the buyer and if you were not aware of the required additional contribution because you did not bother to read the limited partnership agreement and certificate of limited partnership, you would still be liable for the additional contribution. Therefore, if you are going to purchase the interest of a limited partner in an existing syndicate, be very sure that you have a copy of the limited partnership agreement and a copy of the recorded certificate, and that you read and analyze them both line by line. That is the only way in which you can make an accurate determination of what potential liabilities you might face and what restrictions have been placed on the partnership interest you are purchasing.

TAX ATTRIBUTES

In addition to prescribing the respective rights, benefits, and obligations of the partners, the partnership agreement, if properly drafted, protects the tax benefits of your investment. The important advantage of partnerships is that the tax deductions and benefits of the investment flow directly to the investors. The partnership, unlike a corporation, is not a taxpaying entity. However, in recent years, the Internal Revenue Service has attacked limited partnerships in an attempt to classify them as corporations for tax purposes. When such attacks are successful, the tax benefits do not flow directly to the investors, but, rather, are available only to the partnership entity itself, which has no need for them. Be sure that your partnership agreement includes tax provisions that conform to the current Internal Revenue Service regulations. These provisions will ensure that the partnership will be treated as a partnership and not as a corporation for tax purposes. If the syndicator does not provide you with an independent attorney's tax opinion about the partnership's tax status, ask your own attorney to review and assess the agreement's tax provisions.

CONCLUDING COMMENT

I am sure by now the importance of the partnership agreement is readily apparent. If you are seriously considering investing in a particular syndicate, it would be well worth your time to read carefully the terms and provisions of the partnership agreement to make sure it adequately safeguards your investment and conforms with the promises the syndicator has made.

12

Investor Guarantees: Evaluating Syndicator Guarantees

Syndicators, if they are to be financially successful, must know how to structure their syndicates soundly, how to choose sound real estate, how to run it efficiently, and how to sell it for maximum profit. But syndicators, if they are to *survive,* need to understand, above all, the motivations that persuade investors to hand over their money.

There was a time (which more than one syndicator remembers as the "good old days"), when the all-important motivation was fairly simple, if not downright rudimentary. Investors contributed capital to a syndicate because they were attracted by promise of a high economic return on their money.

But all too often a syndicator's promise that "you'll make a bundle" (or whatever more sophisticated financial jargon served to convey the optimistic forecast) was to go unfulfilled. Worse, many unfortunate investors found the notice that potential returns were much lower than anticipated accompanied by a plea for additional capital to keep the syndicate afloat. Smart investors began to stray away from real estate syndicates.

But smarter syndicators (those truly in tune with the investor mind) were not to be dissuaded. To bring the recalcitrant back into real estate, many syndicators began to market their syndicate investments by *guaranteeing* certain returns. For example, that the investor would receive cash distributions even if the property were not to make money.

Lured by these warranties, many investors did bring their money back to real estate syndicates.

But, the next round of unpleasant surprises was not long in coming. Investors have found that some syndicators have been making guarantees that are often unrealistic, sometimes fraudulent. And, like investors of years gone by, they are finding that they too are being asked to contribute additional capital to shore up an investment that is on the edge of collapse.

The lesson many investors are learning anew is simple: if you want a guarantee of success, you should invest in something that is economically sound. Guarantees by the syndicator (or by the builder or seller from whom property is being bought) should never be accepted as the main rationale for investing in a syndicate. The guarantees should not influence your decision to invest or to persuade you to use your capital in a project that, without syndicator guarantees, would be an inferior venture.

That is not to say that all guarantees are meaningless or fraught with dishonesty. And some are clearly needed. But, you should remember that in many projects, the guarantees given you may increase the cost of the investment. The guarantor may have agreed to insure you against certain risks, but at a hidden price. For example, a guarantor may tell you that you will be assured of receiving a predetermined cash flow every year and then jack up the price of the property by an amount that will cover the cost of the guarantee.

Because guarantees must be analyzed carefully, this chapter will help you distinguish between those that have substance and those that may be meaningless. The first part of the chapter explains the basic types of investor guarantees. The second part presents a useful investor guarantee evaluation checklist. The third part analyzes certain investor guarantees in the context of an actual investment situation.

TYPES OF GUARANTEES

Investor guarantees take many forms, depending on the nature of the investment property. The more commonly used guarantees will be discussed.

Cash Flow Guarantees

This guarantee promises that the investor will receive a specified cash return from the investment for a specific period of time; that is, six months, one year, two years, three years, etc. Theoretically, no matter what happens to rental rates, vacancy factors, property taxes, or other expenses, the investor will still receive the cash return.

A modified form of cash flow guarantee is the "negative" cash flow guarantee. In this case, the syndicator promises that the investor will not be asked to contribute additional capital should operational costs exceed income. The syndicator promises to make up the cash deficits from personal funds.

While cash flow guarantees can be clearly beneficial, you should not let them be used to stop you from analyzing the projected revenues and expenses of the property and to determine how much of a cash flow the property generates on its own.

You must keep an eye on "real" cash flow for several reasons. A cash flow guarantee is made for only a specific time. When the guarantee expires, you will be responsible for funding any continuing cash flow deficits. A realistic cash flow analysis, therefore, will help you determine what your future obligations will be. And, you will also know what your immediate obligations might be should the syndicator fail to fulfill the guarantee.

Cash flow, furthermore, is a major factor in the property's resale value. If the cash flow guarantee is funded by the syndicator's own money because the property generates an insufficient cash flow, you could end up losing money if the property cannot be resold at a price that will return your original investment. To ascertain the property's potential market value, you must analyze the projected revenues and expenses, even if you are sure that the syndicator will make good the cash flow guarantee. At the very least, before you invest you should determine whether rentals can be increased during the guarantee period until they are high enough to generate a positive cash flow, to ensure the property's viability after the guarantee expires, and, eventually, to enhance the property's resale value.

Occupancy Guarantees

A modified form of the negative cash flow guarantee is the occupancy guarantee, which is usually made by the builder who is selling a new project to a syndicate. Here, the guarantee calls upon the builder, for example, to manage the property until it is 85 percent full and to fund all operating deficits until that rental goal is reached. Once the 85 percent level is attained, the management of the building and the inherent risks are passed on to the syndicate. Thus, an occupancy guarantee can be beneficial if you are concerned that your syndicator may ask you to make additional capital contributions to meet operational expenses during the time the building is awaiting its full complement of tenants. While there is advantage to taking over a building that is nearly full, you and your syndicate must make sure that the builder has leased the space at realistic rents and terms.

The builder who is committed to an occupancy guarantee and is faced by a potential financial burden as a result, will have a greater incentive to plan, design, and construct the project well enough to draw a full house of tenants in the shortest amount of time possible. The experienced syndicator who has negotiated such a guarantee will insist that the builder secure that guarantee. For example, the syndicator will hold back part of the purchase price until the guarantee is fulfilled.

Rental Rate Guarantees

While there are times that a syndicator will make you guarantees to entice you into an investment, there will also be times when, attracted to but not certain about a project, you may want to ask for certain guarantees.

This may be the case if you are drawn to a syndicate being formed to purchase a new property. Generally, the purchase price of a new apartment building, office complex, or shopping center is based on the builder's or seller's estimate of projected rentals and expenses. Naturally these projections are likely to be very optimistic. If your syndicator is looking to such a project, you may want to ask for a guarantee that the purchase price will indeed reflect the rentals commanded by the property.

You might ask, for example, that the builder's own projections serve as the basis for the guarantee. If the builder projects that the gross annual rental income from the project will be $100,000 and agrees to sell the project on the basis of seven times gross annual rents, the purchase price will be $700,000. If your syndicator feels that the gross multiplier used is reasonable and that the price is therefore reasonable, one factor must still be pinned down: Whether or not the gross annual income will indeed reach $100,000 within a reasonable time. You might consider asking for a guarantee that will assure you that the purchase price of $700,000 will be reduced if rental income does not reach $100,000 by a given date. The guarantee may work this way: If annual rents turn out to be $95,000 rather than $100,000, the purchase price will be reduced by the amount of the differential ($5,000) times the gross multiplier (7)—a total of $35,000.

Construction Cost Guarantees

Should you participate in a new construction syndicate, you must ask also for a guarantee that the builder will absorb any cost overruns, whatever their origin. This is a particularly important guarantee in an inflationary period when construction costs climb continuously. One way to secure the cost guarantee is to require the builder to post an appropriate completion bond. An alternative way to ensure the guarantee will be honored is to retain in escrow a portion of the purchase price until the project is completed.

Sale Leaseback Guarantees

Many syndicates buy a property and then lease it back to the seller. The seller guarantees the syndicate an agreed-upon cash flow during the span of the lease. This arrangement appeals to investors (and may draw you) because at least superficially it does appear to provide some margin of safety to the investment. It assures a given cash flow for the duration of the lease. And, the sale leaseback does tie the seller to the project for an additional length of time. If the seller also happens to be the project's builder, this continuing postsale bond may provide a greater incentive for the seller-builder to develop a quality project.

However, there are pitfalls that should not be overlooked. The seller's ability to comply with the terms of the lease will be determined by the seller's financial resources. If those resources are inadequate or if the seller's liquidity is small, the lease won't be worth much to the syndicate. This is especially true if the syndicate is dealing with a builder whose financial viability and liquidity is entirely dependent on current projects and who is therefore vulnerable to changes in the volatile construction climate.

The sale-leaseback arrangement may also prove worthless if the seller does not have the ability or the staff to manage the project well. And, since the sale-leaseback involves cash flow guarantees, the seller may be tempted to make up for the money that must be paid the syndicate by deferring needed maintenance and repairs on the project and leaving them to the syndicate to carry out after the lease expires.

CHECKLIST

Because you may be offered guarantees and because you may, in some instances, even ask for them, you should have a way of evaluating the worthiness of any promises that are forthcoming. Try to come up with answers to the following questions:

1. *What are the financial resources of the guarantor?*

   Guarantees are only as good as the guarantor's financial resources. Refer to Chapter 3 for suggestions on methods to investigate a syndicator's financial resources. The same criteria can be applied to any other person (builder or seller, for example), who is making you guarantees about your investment.

2. *Who is the guarantor?*

   Is the guarantor an individual who can be held personally liable? Or is the guarantee being made by the syndicator's, builder's, or seller's undercapitalized corporation? This is more than a rhetorical question. I know many syndicators who have formed skelton corporations so that they, as individuals, can avoid personal liability in case their corporations cannot honor their obligations. Therefore, insist on personal guarantees if you are not satisfied that the corporation has sufficient financial resources.

In the case of new construction, there may be two guarantors. One guarantee may be made by the builder of the project to the syndicate partnership. The other guarantee may flow from the syndicator to the syndicate. Both guarantees may overlap and be concurrent, or one may exist without the other. For example, only the builder, and not the syndicator, may guarantee to the syndicate that the project will be finished at a guaranteed cost, occupancy rate, and at a certain rent rate. Should the builder default in these guarantees, your only recourse may be a lawsuit against the builder. Sometimes, however, the syndicator may make exactly the same promises to the syndicate. In that case, you would have recourse against two parties. Thus, if you are to assess the value of a guarantee, you must know who stands behind it.

3. *Are the guarantees in writing?*

Make sure that all guarantees are in writing. Many syndicators use sales personnel who promote the benefits of the investment, including the investment guarantees with a lot of talk. Often overzealous salespeople who work on a commission basis make statements about the investment that are not authorized by the syndicator. If you are tempted by a sales agent's guarantee pitch, be sure you get the offer down on paper.

4. *Has the guarantor given you security for default?*

Whenever possible, try to have the guarantor bind his promises with some kind of secured collateral. You may require that the builder, seller, or syndicator pledge, usually in the form of a second trust deed, whatever equity in the project he or she might have as security that the guarantee will be carried out. Thus, if the guarantor does default, his or her equity is wiped out, thereby in effect reducing the purchase price. (Of course, traditional legal remedies for breach of contract may still be available if necessary.) In addition, since guarantors often have interests in other properties, they may be asked to pledge some of those holdings as security for proper performance of the guarantee. If your syndicator is the guarantor but has no other assets that can be pledged, request that syndication fees serve as security for the guarantee.

5. *Has the guarantor promised to carry out proper maintenance and repair?*

   When a leaseback or cash flow guarantee has been made, be sure that the guarantee agreement requires the guarantor to maintain the property properly, and that the property be turned over to the syndicate at the end of the lease term without major deferred maintenance or replacements requirements.

6. *Have arrangements been made to protect security deposits?*

   Whenever a leaseback (or some similar arrangement) has been made to give you a guarantee on your investment, you should insist that the guarantor, who in turn will lease the individual units in the project, establish a separate security trust fund and that it be placed under the control of the syndicate. The fund will hold the traditional security deposits paid by tenants of an office or apartment building or of any other kind of rental unit. Since tenants are entitled to refunds of their security deposits at the termination of their tenancy, the funds should remain in the trust account. The separate trust fund is necessary because many guarantors use security deposits to cover operating deficits. If a guarantor later defaults on promises made and has used the security deposits as well, the syndicate will have to reimburse the respective tenants as they move out of the premises. Also, when the property is resold, the new buyer is entitled to receive credit for the full amount of security deposits, even if they have been depleted. Thus, your net sales proceeds would also be diminished if steps are not taken to protect the security deposits.

   In other words, you have to be careful because all too

often security deposits, if unprotected, will be used by the guarantor as subsidies to help meet promises; that is, to sustain the guaranteed cash flow, to cover a negative cash flow, or to maintain the property if the guarantor has issued a leaseback agreement.

7. *Can payment of operating expenses be readily verified?*

Any guarantee agreement that provides for the seller to lease back the property should contain assurances that you (or more precisely, your syndicator) will be able to verify and review that the guarantor has made the proper payments for operating expenses. For example, under many leaseback arrangements, it is the guarantor-lessee who will pay the first trust deed payments on behalf of the syndicate. If the syndicate has no way of verifying that those payments are being made on time, the investors may suddenly be surprised to learn that the guarantor is three months behind in payments and that the lender is about to foreclose.

The same precautions are applicable to property taxes. Since property taxes are generally payable only twice a year, a property may seem to be operating profitably; that is, until the time the property taxes are due. Then you find out there are no funds with which to pay them. I would suggest that the lease or guarantee provide for the deposit of property taxes on a monthly basis into an impound account under the control of the syndicate. The same should be true with respect to other major operating expenses, and reserves for repairs and replacements.

8. *Does the guarantor have any financial incentives?*

One of the problems inherent in most guarantees is that they are all stick and no carrot; that is, they threaten, overtly or covertly, all kinds of retribution should the guarantor not live up to the promises made. But they seldom, if ever, include incentives for the guarantor to exceed the minimum performance called for. For example, if you have a promise that the net cash flow from a property will be $20,000 a year, that is exactly what you will get. After all, why should the guarantor try to generate $25,000 in cash if the chances are good that nothing more than a pleasant letter of congratulations will reward the effort.

In fact, you could assume that if a guarantee is not fairly structured, it could actually limit the potential returns from a property investment.

A guarantor should share in the risks, and the rewards as well, on an investment. For example, if the guarantee agreement above were to provide that the guarantor would get 25 percent of all cash flow in excess of $20,000 a year, the guarantor will have considerable incentive to perform as well as possible. The guarantor will probably devote more time and resources to the property, especially if other projects the guarantor is managing do not have similar incentives.

The syndicate, of course, will benefit, and not only because it is receiving a greater cash flow. Don't forget: The greater the cash flow, the greater the value of the property upon resale.

9. *Are there operating reserves?*

One of the best investment guarantees is the creation and existence of adequate operating reserves. Although not technically an investor guarantee, adequate operating reserves are often more useful than many a written warranty. Some syndicators raise just enough money to acquire a property. Thus, there is no room for error. But, if an adequate contingency reserve fund is created, the financial benefits are many. If there are funds in an operating reserve kitty, you can expect that the property will be maintained and operated better than if the syndicator has to run around and raise money every time the roof springs a leak.

Whether or not the contingency reserves are sufficient depends on the nature of the property. For example, new buildings may need higher reserves because some time may pass before occupancy rates and rents are high enough to generate an income that will yield money needed to meet all operating costs on a day-to-day basis. Older properties, however, will need reserves for required repairs and replacements. Consider also the kind of people occupying the building. An adults-only building requires less maintenance than a family-occupied building. The rate of tenant turnover is also a factor. Buildings where tenants come and go after short intervals will have higher repair and maintenance costs than buildings that house a stabler clientele.

If you participate in a sale-leaseback agreement, make sure that there are contingency reserves. These should be maintained separately and be placed under the syndicate's control. Should the lessee default on the guarantee arrangement, the syndicate will have to reassume possession and management of the property. Lessees usually default because they have been unable to cope financially. When a lessee walks away from a property, the financial difficulties inevitably fall into the syndicate's lap. I know of one case in which a builder breached his leaseback contract by not paying property taxes and several mortgage payments. The syndicator immediately moved to retake possession of the property. But there the syndicator was faced with the delinquent property taxes and mortgage payments and had to pay them in order to avoid foreclosure of the property by the mortgage holder. Fortunately, adequate reserves had been established and maintained in an interest-bearing account by the syndicator. These reserves were used to pay the delinquencies and to refurbish common areas of the building and other items of deferred maintenance. Within several months, the building was full, rents were increased, and the building was operating on a profitable basis. No calls for additional capital contributions had to be made. Had the contingency reserves not been available, it is unlikely that the situation could have been turned around soon enough to prevent foreclosure.

Adequate operating reserves, in other words, should be maintained even if the investment features other strong, more explicit, guarantees.

A CASE STUDY

To assist you in evaluting investor guarantees, a syndicate investment containing certain investor guarantees is described below, followed by an evaluation approach that should be applied to your prospective investments.

FOREMOST INDUSTRIAL PROPERTIES, LTD.

> Foremost Industrial Properties, Ltd., is being formed as a limited partnership (the Partnership) for the purpose of acquiring a new 40,000 square foot light industrial building located in Phoenix, Arizona. The purchase price is $950,000, and the cash down payment is $200,000. . . .
>
> The Property has been designed so that it can be readily divided into rentable spaces of either 5,000, 10,000, or 20,000 square feet. Each space will also contain small offices.
>
> The seller of the Property has agreed to manage the Property for the Partnership for the first two years, and has guaranteed that the Partnership will receive $15,000 annually after payment of all expenses, including mortgage payments and property taxes. This equals a 7.5 percent cash return on invested capital. . . .

Let's assume that we are "the Partnership." How meaningful is the guarantee in this investment? To determine this, we must get answers to these questions: Who is the guarantor? What are the seller's abilities and motivations? What is the value of the property? Does written documentation of the guarantee exist? If so, what does it specifically provide? What leasing restrictions, if any, are imposed on the guarantor? Is the guarantee secured? Naturally, other questions may arise, but the answers to the above inquiries would provide you with the basic information you must have to assess the guarantee properly. Let's investigate a little further.

We must know more about the seller-guarantor. For example, what is the person's management experience in similar properties? Has the seller-guarantor managed similar properties, and if so, how did the properties fare? After all, we are leaving our investment in the guarantor's hands during the most important phase of the project, the initial rent-up period. If, at the end of the two-year period, there are undesirable tenants in our building, or if the building has not been properly maintained, there will be considerable trouble. Accordingly, we should ask our syndicator to provide us with specific information regarding the guarantor's management skills, experience, and performance record. If we can, we should also inspect other properties currently managed by the seller.

Is the guarantor an individual, or a corporation? If the guarantor is a corporation, did our syndicator get the personal guarantee of the principal shareholders? If the syndicator has obtained a personal guarantee, is the seller financially capable of meeting the terms of the guarantee if the building remains empty or if the expenses exceed rents? To answer this, we should obtain and review the seller's financial statements.

Why is the seller giving the guarantee in the first place? Perhaps to unload what has proven to be a hard-to-sell building. Perhaps the seller is getting more money for the building than it is worth, or getting a larger down payment than the project would otherwise command.

As we said earlier, investor guarantees often increase the cost of the investment. For example, the guarantor in the above investment may have increased the purchase price and cash down payment by $30,000. That would make up the yearly $15,000 guarantee the seller has made us. On the other hand, we should keep in mind that the seller must still absorb the market risks that low rent might bring, high costs of running the property, and so on. In this case, therefore, even if we assume that the cost of our investment is increased by the guarantee, we may still be well off with the leaseback agreement.

Unfortunately, if we don't know how the guarantor has calculated the property's financial details, we may find it difficult to determine if the guarantee has increased, to an unreasonable extent, the cost of our investment. Thus, to make sure of our venture, we should assess the investment as if it did not come with a guarantee. If we blind ourselves to the insurance offered and compare the project to other similar projects, we might be able to determine if it is overpriced and, if so, by how much.

Guarantees can divert you from making a full evaluation of the investment. You should always determine the investment's fair market value and the expected rents and expenses. After all, even if the guarantee is fulfilled, the syndicate will have to manage the property after the guarantee expires.

In this investment, we should also explore the form and substance of the guarantee given us by the seller. We should make certain the guarantor has executed a written lease or guarantee agreement. We should see a copy of it and make sure it says what has been promised. We must review what provisions have been made for maintaining and repairing the building, and what arrangements have been made for leasing the building. It may be disadvantageous to us if the seller wants to execute short-term leases. After the guarantee expires we may find that our project is plagued by a high vacancy factor because the tenants did not have long-term commitments. Conversely, if the seller-guarantor wants to give long-term leases, we should have some say in the lease provisions. We may want to ask that clauses be inserted that allow, after two years, cost-of-living raises or that limit the syndicate's obligations as landlord once the guarantee expires. The agreement should dictate, in fact, what kind of tenant may occupy the building.

We should also make sure that the seller be prevented from mingling the funds from our property with those funds of other properties under the seller's management. The guarantee should also restrict the seller's ability to enter into long-term maintenance agreements with independent contractors.

Finally, we should find out if there is security against any defaults by the guarantor. For example, if the seller has taken back a second mortgage on the property in connection with the sale, has that mortgage been pledged as security for the full and faithful performance of the guarantee?

CONCLUSION

In summary, investment guarantees can be useful in appropriate cases, expecially in new construction projects. However, as I have said before, you should not let the guarantees blind you to the underlying economic merits or risks of the investment. Nor should you forget that guarantees usually increase the cost of the investment. And, finally, that you must always take time to determine whether the guarantees are indeed meaningful.

13

Investor Rights and Remedies

Let's for the moment assume the worst. Maybe you skipped some of the chapters in this book and ignored the advice in the rest. Or, maybe you followed conscientiously and carefully all of the suggestions I have made, but still, somehow, wound up in a mess. In any case, here you are with a deteriorating investment on your hands.

And so you ask yourself: "What do I do now?"

To answer, at least in part, that woeful question, this chapter will provide you with a broad outline of the investor rights, remedies, and strategies available to you in most investment situations. You will notice that I have hedged the description of the chapter's content. And for good reason. Your precise legal rights and remedies will depend on the specific circumstances of your investment. The proper course of action open to you should your investment suddenly turn to quicksand can be best determined by your own attorney.

To give you the basic understanding you need to assess your situation (and, for that matter, to ask your attorney the right questions and to be able to follow whatever answers you get), let's examine some investments that could lead to disaster.

INVESTMENT A

Three years ago you invested in a syndication that purchased an apartment building in another state. For the first two years of the investment you received regular quarterly cash distributions from the syndicator. You also received annual tax returns and status reports from the syndicator covering the investment. However, in the third year of the investment, the cash distribution for the first quarter of the year did not show up. You became somewhat concerned, and telephoned the syndicator to inquire about the investment. Your first few calls were not returned. You then wrote a letter to the syndicator expressing your concern. As a result, one of the syndicator's sales agents telephoned you and advised you that everything was "going okay," and the syndicator had just decided to accumulate available cash for operational reserves. You accepted this explanation. But now, the due date for the second quarter distribution has come and gone, and no check has graced your mailbox.

Analysis

What should you do? Unfortunately, many investors will do nothing, probably assuming that cash distributions will start again in a subsequent quarter. To be sure, there may not be anything wrong with the investment, and the syndicator's explanation may be valid. However, the pause in cash distributions may be a clue that the apartment building may not be doing well.

Without a doubt, you should start a hard-nosed personal investigation immediately. I would suggest you ask the syndicator to send you operating statements for the property, covering at least the previous six months. Every syndicator should have such statements readily available. Analyze the statements yourself if you are able, or take them to your accountant or lawyer. A proper study of the material should enable you (or your advisers) to pinpoint specific problems and detect any adverse trends. In analyzing the monthly expenditures, be sure to add in accrued expenses which may not be payable yet; property taxes, for example, which are usually paid twice a year and insurance premiums which are typically paid annually. Look out for unusual expenditures, such as excessive repairs and maintenance items, loans or advances to unknown persons or companies, or excessive management fees. See if funds from your property have been pooled with funds from more than one of the syndicator's investments. That means the syndicator may be using your money to fund other projects. You should ask for information concerning the occupancy rate, turnover rate, and rental rates, if such information is not included in the reports. This will enable you to determine whether the rental market has softened. Low occupancy or high turnover rate may also tell you that mismanagement may be a factor.

If the apartment building is now operating consistently on a negative cash flow or deficit basis, further inquiries are warranted. For example, are there sufficient operating reserves to cover the deficits? What is the syndicator doing to increase revenues and/or to reduce expenses? How is the building being maintained? How much time is the syndicator personally devoting to the management of the property? Are demographic changes affecting the property? Getting the answers to some of these questions may require a personal visit to the property.

After you determine the source of the problem, you must then determine whether the problem is temporary, or whether it is likely to continue. If you feel that the problem is more than temporary and may be due to the syndicator's mismanagement of the investment, you should start discussing the matter with the other investors. Investor unity is extremely important in reviving a deteriorating investment. Most syndications involve investors who have no prior business or personal relationships with each other and are strangers to each other. Thus, the investors often work independently and, thereby, unintentionally impede each other. Therefore, when problems are detected, you must organize properly and early, usually through investor meetings. If you and your fellow investors can proceed on a common, unified front, and the syndicator is aware of the unity, you stand a much better chance of solving the investment problems.

If you have reason to believe that the investment is in trouble and that the syndicator is at the root of the problem, you should give early consideration to removing the syndicator. Your partnership agreement should include the necessary removal procedures. However, there are certain risks you should consider before you get the impeachment ball rolling. First, should you succeed in ousting your syndicator, you and your fellow investors will have to find a competent person or company to assume the former general partner's duties and to manage the syndicate. Finding an adequate substitute is not an easy thing to do.

Should the search for a substitute manager be unsuccessful, your investment, of course, may deteriorate even more quickly. Moreover, without the syndicator as general partner, the limited partnership may, in the eyes of the law, be considered a general partnership. This in turn may result in personal liability for you and the other investors. Accordingly, if you are going to remove the syndicator, make sure that careful plans are made and carried out first.

INVESTMENT B

You invested in a citrus property syndication three years ago, primarily because of the favorable tax shelter aspects of the investment. The partnership agreement required the investors to make annual contributions of $4,000 per investment unit. All along, you had been receiving appealing annual reports from the syndicator describing the new developments in the area immediately adjacent to the property, as well as expressions of interest by prospective purchasers of the property. Recently, however, you received a letter from the syndicator stating that several of the investors defaulted in their annual contributions. Pursuant to the terms of the partnership agreement, the interests of the defaulting partners were being offered to you and the other nondefaulting investors in return for contributing the required capital. You decided that you do not wish to sink more into the investment. But, last week, you received another letter informing you that none of the defaulting partners' interests had been purchased. As a result, the property taxes and mortgage payments are in arrears because capital contributions were insufficient. You attempt to contact the syndicator to find out what's happening, but your calls are being evaded. You next decide to take it upon yourself to visit the syndicator personally and find out what is going on. The syndicator is nowhere to be found, and only one secretary is in the office. The secretary advises you that foreclosure of the property is eminent. Further investigation reveals that the syndicator has been taking substantial management fees during this time. To boot, it turns out the syndicator was the seller of the property to your syndicate. The sale was handed through a double escrow at a substantially marked-up price. In other words, he made a bundle on your syndicate.

Analysis

What should you do in the above situation? Here, more so than in the prior example, it is important that you organize the other investors as soon as possible, and proceed on a united front. You must remove the syndicator quickly as manager of your investment and notify the bank where the investment accounts are maintained that the syndicator no longer has authority to make disbursements from the accounts. You should concurrently contact the mortgagee who is considering, or pursuing, foreclosure, and explain what has transpired, and request some kind of a temporary moratorium. Explain that the syndicator has violated a trust relationship and fiduciary obligations to the investors, that the syndicator was therefore removed, that you and your other investors were taking over management of the investment, and as soon as you are organized, all obligations will be fully satisfied.

You must then determine promptly whether the property itself has sufficient value to justify the investment of additional funds. This usually requires an appraisal of the property's market value and comparing that value to the outstanding obligations of the investment. If the amount of the obligations is equal to or greater than the price the property conceivably might bring, you should, in plain language, bail out, unless you have strong indications that the property will appreciate in value.

Whatever your decision, you still must decide if you want to take legal action against the syndicator. In this case, there seems to be ample grounds for a lawsuit. From the very moment you signed the syndicate agreement, your syndicator had a legally recognized duty (a so-called fiduciary duty) to the syndicate's investors. The fiduciary duty is broad: The syndicator has to avoid misconduct that would compromise your interests. More important, the fiduciary duty imposes on the syndicator an obligation to act in a positive fashion to protect, preserve, and promote your interests.

Your syndicator violated his fiduciary duties in wholesale fashion. He did not keep you properly informed about the property. He did not disclose to you that the property was sold to the syndicate at a substantial markup. Finally, he obviously acted directly against your interests by paying himself management fees at a time when the syndicate did not have sufficient funds to meet mortgage payments.

If a syndicator, in good faith, has at times merely made bad business decisions, you won't have legal recourse to compensate you for the adverse effects of those dealings. However, further digging into the syndicator's conduct may yield breaches of fiduciary duty. The syndicator may have personally used the syndicate's assets or might have diverted a potential beneficial opportunity away from the syndicate to his own personal benefit.

You can be sure that the syndicator's conduct or transactions with the syndicate will be rigorously scrutinized by the courts. If the syndicator cannot prove that he acted in good faith and the court determines he has indeed breached his fiduciary duty, you will be entitled to compensation for any damages you have sustained as a result. If the syndicator's misconduct is sufficiently reprehensible, the court may even award punitive damages.

INVESTMENT C

Almost two years ago you and 35 other people invested in a syndicate to acquire a seven-story office building located in Long Beach, California. The syndicate paid $2.5 million, and made a $500,000 cash down payment. You were lured into the project because the syndicator's offering circular projected that the investment would generate an 8 percent annual cash return for the investors, and that the tax write-offs for the first two years of the investment would be 40 percent and 33 percent, respectively. However, the first year's cash return has turned out to be only 2 percent. Worse, you have just received notice that the Internal Revenue Service is auditing the investment. The Internal Revenue Service, moreover, is attempting to classify the partnership as a corporation for tax purposes. If the Internal Revenue Service succeeds, you could lose all prior and future tax write-offs from the investment. Naturally, you are quite displeased about the turn of events. You approach the syndicator and ask that he repurchase your investment interest because you feel the investment was not correctly represented to you. Although the syndicator regrets what has happened, he tells you frankly that he does not wish to purchase your interest.

Analysis

What possible recourse do you have against the syndicator? You don't think that the syndicator intentionally misrepresented the investment's potential. Nevertheless, you still feel misled. Not all may be lost, however. Even though the syndicator won't accommodate you, you might still look to the state and federal securities statutes for possible remedies.

Syndicators must comply with stringent federal and state securities statutes covering the offer and sale of syndicate investment interests. Even though your syndicator may have acted in good faith in offering and selling the syndicate investment interests, you may have proper legal grounds for the full return of your investment, if the syndicator has failed to comply with the applicable statutes.

As we discussed in Chapter 2, at the core of state and federal regulations are requirements that a syndicator register an investment offering unless the offering is exempt from the appropriate registration requirements. In the case of your syndicate, you know that there are 36 investors and that the syndicator raised substantial capital since the purchase of the office building required a $500,000 down payment.

You should, therefore, make three important inquiries.

1. Did the syndicator register with the appropriate federal and/or state regulatory agencies? The offering circular should reveal if the offering was registered.

2. If the syndicator did not register the syndication, was it because the syndicate fell under one of the appropriate exemptions? Remember that under state and federal laws, there

are several circumstances under which a failure to register is legally sanctioned. But also remember that you have to check thoroughly because the syndicate may be exempt from federal registration requirements, but not the state's or, perhaps, vice versa. In any case, this is a highly technical area and you should seek the guidance of an attorney.

3. Do you still have time to take legal action? The securities statutes have specific statute of limitations periods, after which no legal suit may be filed against the syndicator. The statute of limitations for the federal registration statute is only one year from the date of violation, and therefore your federal rights appear to have expired. The statute of limitations for state securities statutes, however, varies from state to state. Fortunately for you, the statute of limitations for the California registration requirements is two years from the date of violation or one year after discovery of the violation, whichever first expires. Thus under California law you still have time to take legal action for any violation of California's registration requirements.

Registration requirements notwithstanding, you might be able to avail yourself of statutes designed to prevent fraud in the securities field. In general, these statutes prohibit a syndicator from making affirmative misrepresentations of material facts or from omitting material facts in connection with the offer and sale of the syndicate interests. These statutes are interpreted liberally in favor of the investors. Violations of these statutes generally entitle investors to a full refund of their entire investment, plus interest, and in some cases, even punitive damages. However, in your investment, it may be difficult to prove that the syndicator has violated an antifraud statute. The syndicator's failure to meet projected cash flow may not give you sufficient grounds to claim fraud, unless you can establish that the syndicator had information that an 8 percent projection would be clearly unrealistic. Does the fact that the IRS has attacked the tax classification of the syndicator mean that his representations about tax write-offs were fraudulent? Only if you can establish that the syndicator took unreasonable tax risks in structuring the syndicate. In any event, you might raise the specter of these potential statutory violations to help you to negotiate effectively with the syndicator for a return of your invested capital. However, you should be sure that your attorney has checked the applicable statute of limitations period for the applicable statutes you want to invoke when you meet the syndicator.

INVESTORS STRATEGY CHECKLIST

As the examples above have emphasized, planning and strategy are important when you are attempting to salvage what appears to be a deteriorating investment. You will now find a discussion of additional rescue strategies that may be appropriate, depending on the particular nature and status of your investment.

1. Before you make any formal demands of the syndicator, you should attempt to gather as much documentation and information as possible concerning your investment. For example, you may wish to review the syndicator's books and records concerning the operation of the investment property. You should also attempt to obtain a written statuts report about the investment from the syndicator. You should proceed cautiously, however, because once the syndicator is aware of your suspicions, you are not likely to receive much cooperation.

2. As soon as you suspect there are problems, ask your attorney to assess your position and your potential legal claims. Once you have sound legal advice, you can put your demands to the syndicator, presenting as much documentation as possible. Chances are that the syndicator, concerned that word will spread to other investors and that other syndicate investment opportunities may be affected, will be willing to negotiate. A satisfactory resolution at an early stage may result.

3. If you are unable to negotiate a satisfactory settlement, you must then determine whether a suit should be filed against the syndicator. Frequently, promoters of a failed syndication will also be insolvent. Therefore, even though you may have appropriate legal causes of action, your efforts against the syndicator may simply not be worthwhile because legal action may cost you more than you can expect to recoup. Therefore, determine whether other parties—people with some financial resources—might be involved and liable. Depending on the nature of the syndication itself, you might be able to sue and

collect from the accountants who certified the financial statements of the syndicator and the annual operational statements, the attorneys who may have drafted the prospectus or offering circular for the syndicator, and other experts (such as real estate appraisers) whose opinions were included in the prospectus and were instrumental in persuading you to invest. Many times syndicators use sales agents to solicit funds from the investors. They should also be considered as potential targets for a lawsuit.

4. Look for multiple syndicators. Many times there are several syndicators involved in the same investment. I know of a case in which one syndicator purchased the investment property and resold it to a second syndicator. He in turn, resold the property to a group of investors. The sales and resales included multiple markups of syndication fees, which were not fully disclosed to the final investors. The investors filed an action against both syndicators. The syndicator who sold the property directly to them was insolvent. However, because the first syndicator had sufficient funds, the investors were able to recover their money from him.

5. If there seems to be grounds for a lawsuit against the syndicator, you must decide whether to bring an individual action on your own behalf, or a class action on behalf of all the investors. The decision about the type of legal action may depend upon the size of your investment and the number of investors involved. Because of ever-increasing litigation costs, it may not pay for you to bring an action by yourself because, even though the action may be successful, the cost of prosecuting it may be too expensive. On the other hand, if you and a few other individuals are involved, it may be worthwhile for you to institute an action jointly, rather than to file a class action. There are disadvantages to class action suits. A class action suit requires court approval of any settlement, and to obtain approval you must comply with stringent court requirements; for example, that all investors be notified, that most approve the settlement that you have settlement hearings, and so on. Therefore, class action proceedings become time consuming and very expensive, and make settlements difficult. Class action cases require that all members of the class, or in this case, all investors, participate equally in the benefits of the settlement or

recovery. Many times, the syndicator will not have sufficient assets to satisfy fully the demands of all the investors and therefore, the investors will receive only a pro rata portion of any recovery or settlement. Thus, the potential recovery may be larger when an individual or joint action with several investors is pursued.

Class actions, on the other hand, do have certain important advantages. First, they entail considerably higher legal expenses for the syndicator. Therefore, to avoid lengthy and costly litigation, the syndicator may be willing to settle the case at an earlier stage or for a larger amount of money. In addition, class action cases are handled by attorneys on behalf of plaintiffs on a contingent fee basis. Thus, your out-of-pocket expenditure will be considerably less than in an individual action. In any event, just the threat of a class action suit can prove useful in negotiations for settlement with the syndicator. The specter of a broad class action suit may motivate a syndicator to settle with one or a few investors, rather than face a challenge by *all* the investors.

6. You might also consider filing a formal complaint with state and/or federal securities regulatory agencies. However, there are inherent risks in such procedures. First, these agencies quite often seek and obtain only cease and desist orders that prohibit the syndicator from further violations. This will not help if you already have been burned. Further, if the cease and desist order forces the syndicator out of business, how will he be able to make restitution?

7. Practice preventive medicine—keep well informed about your investment. I once represented an investor who became suspicious of several investments he had made with the same syndicator because the investor felt he was not receiving complete information concerning the status of his investments. After appropriate inquiry and investigation, his suspicions were confirmed. He found evidence of widespread fraud on the part of the syndicator. We demanded that the syndicator return the investor's entire capital plus interest. Because we moved quickly, at a time when the syndicator was still quite solvent, he made a quick settlement with my client on our terms. When the other investors finally discovered the same

problems, the syndicator could not afford to honor their demands for the return of their money.

CONCLUSION

There is a broad spectrum of potential legal and practical remedies available today to investors in deteriorating syndications. The courts have imposed high standards of professional responsibility on syndicators in an effort to protect the interests of syndicate investors. However, only careful factual investigation, planning and timely action will help guarantee maximum satisfaction.

14

A Review of Syndicate Investment Strategies: Some Dos, Don'ts, and Caveats

The purpose of this chapter is to underline some important syndicate strategies and policies you must adopt to give at least minimal guarantees to your investment. Some of these points we discussed before. Some are new. But for lack of a better term, I am simply calling them some dos, some don'ts, and some caveats. The advice is based primarily upon my experience in representing both syndicators and syndicate investors. I have seen many investors lose their money because they made simple and basic mistakes that could have been easily avoided through proper safeguard procedures.

SOME DOS

Make Sure Everything Is in Writing

Syndicate investments are usually promoted through meetings, telephone conversations, and other face-to-face contacts among investors, syndicators, and syndicate sales agents. As a result, many syndicate investors base their investment decisions on verbal, rather than written, statements and representations. It is not surprising, therefore, that disputes later arise over what was said or not said by the syndicator or the syndicator's representatives. The only way to really avoid the disputes and disappointments are to insist that all material investment representations be repeated clearly in writing, either in an offering brochure, partnership agreement, or other appropriate legal document.

It is particularly important that you insist on written documents when you are dealing with sales agents for a syndicator. Typically, agents, who are working on a commission basis, will overstate the investment benefits, or even misstate the investment benefits, in making their presentation. Accordingly, you should make sure that all the promises made by sales personnel are also contained in the written investment documents. If the syndicator or sales agents refuse to put any representations in black and white, you have immediate warning to steer clear. Just as important, if the promises are written out but do not come true, you will have a basis on which to build a claim that the syndicator breached a contract made with you, breached fiduciary duties, or simply engaged in fraud. Without written agreements, it would simply be your word against the syndicator's.

Obtain Legal Documents

Most syndicators will offer you only a copy of the partnership agreement and the offering brochure or circular. However, you should not be satisfied with only these materials. If you are to make sure that the information in the offering brochure (or in any other written communication from the syndicator) is accurate, you should obtain and review certified copies of the escrow instructions, the purchase contract for the property (if a contract is used), the title policy, the grant deed, the promissory notes issued in connection with the sale, and the trust deeds or mortgages. The trust deeds or mortgages and promissory notes are especially important if an all-inclusive trust deed is to be used. Only by analyzing *all* of these documents can you be sure that the syndicator has been leveling with you.

Meet Your Syndicator

Always personally meet the syndicator before making an investment. You should do this even if you participate in a large public syndication. After all, it is the syndicator who is the motivating factor behind the success or failure of your syndicate investment. You are relying on that person's skill, experience and expertise in the selection, negotiation, and management of your investment property. Accordingly, you should meet and size up the syndicator. You should also use the opportunity to have the syndicator verify any promises made by sales agents. Do not simply rely on fancy resumés describing the syndicator's background. Question the syndicator closely on key points in the resumé.

If you are dealing with a corporate syndicator, don't be afraid to ask to see the president. If the president of the corporation doesn't have time to see you, you should pass on the investment.

Personally Inspect the Property

There is no substitute for a firsthand inspection of the investment property. If you rely only on the investment information and figures presented to you by the syndicator or a sales agent, you will be doing yourself a disservice. By checking the investment property yourself and comparing it with similar properties in the immediate area, you can form your own opinion about the property's investment potential. You may even see things that the syndicator has overlooked in evaluating the property's investment potential.

Make Sure the Syndicate Has Legal and Record Title to the Property

Many properties are sold through contracts of sale or conditional sales contracts. In these contracts, legal title to the property is not immediately conveyed to the purchaser. Reasons for using these contracts vary. In some states they may be used to prevent a first trust deed holder from accelerating the loan, thereby maintaining a favorable interest rate. Or the seller may insist on this arrangement as a way of retaining legal title as additional security for payment of the balance of the purchase price by the buyer.

Often, these contracts are not recorded. As a result, the purchasing syndicate has no interest of record in the property whatsoever. Unrecorded ownership creates numerous risks for your investment. For one thing, the syndicate cannot obtain title insurance to protect its ownership interest. Furthermore, the property could actually be resold by the original seller without the syndicate's knowledge, and the investors could end up without a property. I am even aware of situations where the original sellers have foreclosed against syndicate properties without warning the syndicator or the investors, thereby effectively denying them the opportunity to protect their ownership interest. As a result, the investors lost their complete investment. Had the contract of sale been recorded, they would have received legal notice of the sellers' attempt to foreclose and would have had a chance to prevent the action.

Consequently, you should insist that all property ownership changes be made through a recorded grant deed or a purchase agreement in the name of the purchasing syndicate. This will give you and the syndicate legal protection against secret foreclosures and other transactions affecting your property rights. A properly recorded sale will allow the syndicate to obtain title insurance necessary to guarantee that your syndicate has good legal title to the property. You should also ask for a copy of the escrow instructions to verify that the syndicate will get legal title to the property. Later get a copy of the deed or other recorded instrument that gives evidence of title.

Find out Who Is the Seller of the Property

Some offering brochures do not disclose the name of the seller of the property. This may be due to oversight or it may be intentional. You should always ask for the name of the seller. You should also inquire what the seller's financial relationship, if any, is to the syndicator. For example, the seller may be a corporation in which the syndicator is an officer, director, or shareholder. You want to avoid conflicts of interest that will work against you—not to mention situations in which sales commissions become hidden syndication fees.

Sometimes the syndicator will buy a property and then resell it to the syndicate. Such a practice can lend itself to abuse because, by its very nature, it is not an arm's length transaction. For example, the syndicator, on resale, may be marking up the price beyond the property's fair market value. Accordingly, if you find the syndicator is the seller, you will want to scrutinize closely the transaction to determine whether the syndicator is making a hidden or undisclosed profit.

In fact, you should also ask how long the seller has owned the property. If the seller has only owned it a short time (let's say six months or less) you are probably facing a back-to-back purchase. And this is also a good indication that your purchase price has been inflated.

Keep Informed about Your Investment

One of the greatest sources of syndicate investment risk is investor laziness. Too many investors forget about their investment after they have handed over their initial contributions. For some strange reason, many investors are almost indifferent about their investment. They presume that the syndicator will take care of everything. All they have to do, they think, is sit back and collect the profits or take advantage of the tax benefits. While this may be true in most syndicate investments, it can prove financially disastrous in many.

I cannot overemphasize the importance of keeping well informed regarding the progress of your investment. You or your attorney or accountant should make periodic reviews because they can result in early detection of investment problems. When you spot a potential problem early, you can move to avert financial disaster later on. Also, if the syndicator is aware of your continued interest, he may be stimulated to be more conscientious in managing your investment.

It is also a good idea to request that the syndicator hold periodic investor meetings and issue investor status reports. This will enable you and your fellow investors to get to know each other, thereby creating unity which can be very beneficial should problems vis-à-vis the syndicator arise later. The more unified the investor group is, the more quickly it can act to prevent or mitigate problems concerning the investment. It is, therefore, also a good idea to compile a list of every investor's current mailing address, should you need to contact each other quickly.

Get the Syndicator to Invest in the Property

As discussed previously, the greater the financial interest of the syndicator in the property, the greater the incentive to the syndicator to select, negotiate, and manage the property properly. Therefore, whenever possible, try to get the syndicator to invest personal funds on the same terms and conditions as you do. Failing that, try to get the syndicator to take a portion of the syndication fees by way of an equity interest in the property, rather than front-end cash fee. Such a syndicate structure assures mutuality of interest between the syndicator and investors.

Seek Independent Counsel Concerning Your Investment

Much of the advice discussed in this book will enable you to make a basic, sound analysis of prospective syndicate investments. Hopefully, the various points made will enable you to screen prospective investments so that you differentiate among good, mediocre, and poor investments. However, once you have completed your own investment analysis and screening process, you should ask your attorney to review the legal and tax aspects of the investment before you actually commit your capital. Many times, your attorney can point out risks or deficiencies in the investment that you may have overlooked or to which you may not have given enough importance.

Request Complete Partnership Tax Returns

You should request that the syndicator send you, every year of the investment, copies of the complete partnership tax return the syndicate must file with the Internal Revenue Service. This return, branded 1065-K, contains very useful information about the partnership's financial affairs, including a profit-and-loss statement, a balance sheet, and a list with the names and addresses of all the investors. A careful review of the return should enable you to detect existing or potential problems in the investment. If you can't make sense of it, have your accountant look at the return. If you are uncertain about anything you discover or feel that there are ambiguities in the return, investigate immediately.

Be sure, by the way, that you get 1065-K in answer to your specific response. The syndicator may give you a K-1 form. However, you are entitled to receive a K-1 in any case because it is the form that includes information you need for your own tax returns. That information, however, is limited and tells you nothing about the partnership's overall operations.

SOME DON'TS

Don't Wait until the End of the Year to Invest

Most investors wait until the last few months of the year before selecting their syndicate investments because come November and December they suddenly become tax conscious and aware that they should pay attention to their tax planning needs. As a result, they make a mad scramble for syndicate investments and, in the process, make hasty investment and ill-advised decisions. Furthermore, many sellers of properties are aware of the year-end rush. As a result, they usually jack up the price of their properties.

As silly as year-end investment decisions are, there was a time when there was some justification for considering them because prepaid interest (which was a feature of many investment opportunities) was tax deductible for the current year, even if the investment was made on December 31. However, the Tax Reform Act of 1976 wiped out prepaid interest as a tax deductible item.

Remember too that the 1976 Tax Reform Act allows you a depreciation write-off only for the period of time during which you held an interest in the building. You can no longer buy into a syndicate in December and claim tax allowances for the entire year. Thus, you have one more reason to invest as early in the year as possible.

All in all, you must keep in mind that your investment decision should be made on the basis of facts that are independent of the calendar.

Don't Invest too Much with the Same Syndicator

You are considering syndicate investment to diversify and to expand your property ownership. At a very basic level, investing with different syndicators serves to diversify your interests even further.

But there is also a measure of insurance that comes with investments made in different syndicates. Even if you have confidence in one syndicator, putting all your capital in the hands of one person is to court disaster. The syndicator may run into bad luck, and also may stretch thin managerial and financial resources. Worse, the syndicator you trusted so implicitly at the beginning may simply be a crook. I know of one case (certainly not an isolated instance) in which investors, year after year, placed their capital with the same syndicator. At first, the man met their every expectation; that is, made good on cash flow promises, and returned gratifying profits on invested capital. But then, the checks stopped coming. When some investors began to ask questions, the man's financial empire collapsed, revealing a massive fraud. The syndicator had been using capital contributed by one group of investors to make good on promises made to other investors. But in time he was unable to lure enough capital to meet his pyramiding obligations. Investors who had given him all their capital because he had performed so spectacularly when they first joined with him found themselves close to ruin.

Don't Be the First Investor to Put up Your Money

Before actually making your investment in a particular investment, make sure that the syndicator is raising money from other investors as well. Don't be the first investor to contribute your capital. Make sure the syndicator has the ability to raise the required capital to acquire and properly maintain the property. Don't be pressured by a syndicator or a sales agent who may tell you that if you don't put up your money right away, the syndication may soon be oversubscribed.

Don't Allow Commingling of Syndicate Funds

Many syndicate partnership agreements allow the syndicator to commingle the funds of various syndications, although separate accountings are to be maintained. This is a precarious practice and has often resulted in investment losses. Some syndicators will shift money from one syndicate to another if the second one is unsound or runs into trouble. At some point, however, too many troubled investments will cause otherwise viable investments to suffer, or even fail. I have even seen some syndicators borrow money from their syndications for personal use.

Consequently, you should always insist that your syndicate's funds be maintained only in separate accounts in the syndicate's name, and that such funds may only be used for the syndicate's benefit. This restriction should be written into the syndicate partnership agreement. To make sure that the funds are indeed in the syndicate's name, not in the syndicator's name, ask for periodic bank statements.

Don't Buy from, or Sell to, a Related Syndicate

Some syndicators form new syndicates to buy properties from their existing syndicates. This practice is rife with potential conflicts of interest and can only work to your disadvantage. For one thing, how can there be effective and advantageous negotiations on price or terms of sale if the syndicator is representing both the buying and selling syndicate? Accordingly, you should not invest in a syndicate that is buying a property from one of your syndicator's other syndicates, and you should not approve of any sale by your syndicate to another syndicate formed by your syndicator.

SOME CAVEATS

Be Careful about Investing after the Property Has Been Acquired

Many syndicators purchase a property for their syndicate, close escrow, and go on seeking and accepting capital from additional investors.

However, if you join a syndicate that has already acquired a piece of property, you will obtain tax benefits only from the day you join, not the date the property was acquired. Tax law requires an allocation of tax benefits for the period of time in which you are an investor. Accordingly, if a property is acquired by a syndicate on November 1, and you contribute your capital to the syndicate on December 1, you will get only one month's depreciation benefits while other investors are entitled to two months worth of tax benefits. You, after all, owned your interest for only one half the portion of the calendar year in which the property was owned by the syndicate. The tax law does not allow you a retroactive allocation of the tax losses. This is true even though the syndicator may have told you otherwise. Therefore, if you want to maximize your tax benefits, make sure that your capital is invested before the syndicate acquires the property.

Also, you should be certain that you and other latecomer investors have not acquired 50 percent or more of the partnership interests after the property has been bought. A sale of 50 percent of the interests in a syndicate within a 12-month period could trigger unfavorable changes in the tax benefits available to the partnership. Many a syndicator, hot on the trail of a good property will personally buy 50 percent of the partnership interests just so escrow can be closed. Then, the syndicator will resell those interests to new investors. If you get caught in a situation like this, you may very well find that the tax benefits you expected do not materialize or do not live up to your expectations.

Be Careful about High Debt Service Investments

As a general rule, you should not select properties that have high debt service ratios, unless you are willing to incur higher risks and are confident that other factors make the investment worthwhile. Whenever the debt service ratio (percentage of loan payments to gross income) exceeds 50 percent, it will be extremely difficult to operate the property on a cash break-even basis. Thus, if you are going to select an investment with a high debt service, you should satisfy yourself that rentals can easily be increased to offset the unfavorable financing. Further, you should make sure that sufficient operating reserves are maintained by the syndicator to cover any operating deficits until rents can be increased.

Be Careful about Apartment Investments Where the Landlord Pays for Tenant Utilities

Because of our so-called energy crisis, utility expenses in income properties have skyrocketed in recent years. Office building and commercial property leases usually include clauses that permit increased costs to be passed on to the tenants. Most newer apartment buildings have separate utility meters for each unit and tenants assume the relevant costs.

However, some apartment buildings have a single master meter. Therefore, the owner-landlord is required to pay the utilities. As a result, the owner has to absorb most of the substantial increases in utility rates because it is difficult to pass all of these extra costs on to tenants through rent increases. Further, there is little incentive for tenants to practice energy conservation. As a result, these properties generally cannot operate nearly as economically as properties where tenants pay their own utilities. Therefore, you should be extremely cautious when you are considering an apartment investment where the landlord is required to pay for tenant utilities.

Be Careful about Apartment Investments That Cannot Afford Full-Time Resident Managers

One of the primary advantages of syndicate investments is the opportunity afforded you to acquire interests in projects that can pay for better management services. Larger apartment buildings can afford full-time resident managers, whereas, small apartment buildings often cannot.

Buildings with full-time resident managers are usually much better maintained and managed than properties that cannot afford full-time resident managers. Therefore, it is usually best to avoid investments in smaller properties unless you are satisfied that proper management can be provided.

Be Careful about Split Installment Syndications

More and more syndications are structured so that investors can make capital contributions on an installment plan spread over several years. By splitting the contribution, each investor can afford to buy a larger share in the investment. Therefore, fewer investors are required. This makes it easier for the syndication to gain classification as a private offering for securities law purposes, and, therefore, to sidestep the registration requirements of the state and federal securities acts. The risk to you in such syndicate structures is that some investors may be unable to meet their additional installments. This risk is magnified in new construction investments because early revenues will be small or, for a while, nonexistent. Accordingly, you should inquire whether the syndicator has access to other sources of capital should some investors default. You should also make sure appropriate penalties can be applied to the investor who defaults. Financial incentives to reward nondefaulting investors who make up the necessary shortages should also be available.

The defaulting investor still has a financial interest in the partnership equal to at least his initial capital contribution. However, the partnership agreement should provide that any investor who defaults on an obligation to the syndicate must sell his interest to the other investors at a reduced price.

Index